getting ready for college

getting
ready for
college

POLLY BERENT

RANDOM HOUSE NEW YORK

RANDOM HOUSE TRADE PAPERBACKS and colophon are
registered trademarks of Random House, Inc.

Portions of this work were previously published
in pamphlets published by the author in 1993
and 1997 entitled *Getting Ready for College*.

Library of Congress Cataloging-in-Publication Data

Berent, Polly.
Getting ready for college / by Polly Berent.
p.   cm.
Includes index.
ISBN 0-8129-6896-4
1. College student orientation—United States.   I. Title.
LB2343.32.B48 2003
378.19'8—dc21   2003041375

Random House website address: www.atrandom.com

Printed in the United States of America

4 6 8 9 7 5 3

Book design by Jennifer Ann Daddio

For

TONY DITTMER

and

KATIE HALL

foreword

Every year, three million incredibly well prepared students enter college. As early as their sophomore year of high school, most of these college freshmen had received their first glossy view book from College A peddling their educational experience as second to none. Most were bombarded with information about applying to and choosing the college that was right for them, and, equipped with excellent, easily accessible resources, they did their own research as well. By the time they actually arrive on campus, most have visited the campus during the summer, attended a fall open house, interviewed, spent a night on campus once admitted, and attended summer orientation.

All of this preparation leads up to the first day of college, when parents (many of whom have been nearly as involved in the process as their offspring) drop off their sons and daughters and wave goodbye. Each student, standing there as the car pulls away, is suddenly aware that there are no handouts or instructional videos offering further information and advice. The parents, meanwhile, are crossing their fingers, hoping their kid will figure it all out.

If this fear seems very real to you, don't be embarrassed. This book was written to address any and all questions freshmen and their parents may have. It answers an unmet need for something more than a CliffsNotes version of what to do once you arrive on campus. You've done yourself a major favor by buying the only survival guide you'll need to successfully avoid possible pitfalls and get through the first year.

This book is not an attempt to marginalize the efforts of student affairs offices across the country. Its mission is to fill in the gaps where even the most robust, detailed student orientation packet may fall short. Offered here is an easy-to-read, step-by-step guide that's got your back from the day you first walk into Wal-Mart to buy those extra-long sheets all the way to your final exams. Simply put, *Getting Ready for College* is a soup-to-nuts resource that will arm both students and their families with the best, most practical insider information available, enabling a seamless transition into college life.

Addressed in this book are the concerns of many students and their families. You'll find list upon list of helpful tips, from how to exercise NATO-like diplomacy skills with your roomie to how to make your crib more than just a place to crash. You'll also find hard-nosed advice on time management, choosing a major, health care, managing finances, writing papers, professors' office hours, building your first loft, and even social life. You will learn not just how to best navigate the process, but also how to avoid indecision, frustration, and wasted time along your route.

If the author's expert advice isn't enough to convince you that this information is essential, take it from current college students and the words of their sworn testimonials. These students are an invaluable resource, as life lessons are seldom found in college view books and you'll be hard pressed to hear about them on a campus tour. It's odd, really, that the stories of the true college experts—the students—are so seldom tapped for their practical insights. Not to worry, though—in this book, the keg is trapped and flowing with the unfiltered opinion of students. No spin doctors here!

A simplified, demystified view of life at college is what students and parents need most, and that is exactly what this book will provide. Remember: for every fear or question you have about college, there's an answer. So equip yourself with the solid, seasoned advice of those who have gone through the process and made it out alive, and you *will* be ready for college.

Robert Franek
Editorial Director, The Princeton Review

contents

introduction

When my son returned from his first year of college, there were many things he wished he had known about beforehand. He got together with his high school friends and told sad tales of how he had had not one but two bikes stolen. They immediately chimed in with their own stories. Many of them had also learned the hard way to cope with all kinds of surprises, both great and small, during their first year on campus.

Thinking that sharing what these kids had learned might provide other college-bound students with brighter and less costly beginnings, I decided to see what else I could discover. What do you wish someone had told you *before* you left for college? Their amazingly open and enthusiastic responses to this question on a wide range of topics—from things to bring to things to think about—are the heart of this guide.

It turned out to be a fascinating project. It was also a lot of fun. So I continued to follow up with these twenty students throughout their college years, and with scores of others long after my son and his friends had graduated.

May you find this collection of individual stories, tips, insights, and hindsights helpful as you prepare for college. I also hope it will provide you and your parents with a realistic view of college life.

Sections on career planning and jobs are more recent additions. They will serve as a resource when you declare a major or choose a career. Going to college is a wonderful and sometimes scary opportunity. It's a time to be on your own, make new friends, explore new ideas, and carve out a niche in a totally new place. However, I hope that along with all this freedom and exploration you will also discover something you want to do when you get out. But first you must begin.

Have a very good year!

Polly Berent

getting ready for college

1.

things to bring

Before you start packing your bags and loading the van, there are two things you should do. First, check to see if your college has mailed you a suggested list of things you will need to bring. If not, many schools provide this kind of information online. Pull up your school's website and click on "residential" or "dormitory housing." You may be able to take a tour of the rooms and check out dimensions. (Think small!) In addition to providing information such as whether you should bring regular or extra-long sheets for your bed, there may be helpful hints about leaving pets and power tools at home.

The second thing to do is to call university housing to find out who your roommate will be.

"It was good to get to know a little bit about him before we actually met. We decided in advance which of us would bring the big items—refrigerator, microwave, TV, fan. By avoiding duplication, we saved both money and valuable room space."

Here's a composite list of what twenty students we interviewed took with them to college.

Caution: In August, many discount and specialty stores feature aisles overflowing with items just for the dorm—all in bright colors, too. Don't get carried away. Remember: Packing for college is an art, not a science. It depends on judgment.

basics

- ❑ clothes
- ❑ lots of clothes hangers
- ❑ socks and underwear
- ❑ baseball cap for bad hair days
- ❑ raincoat or parka/umbrella
- ❑ boots (rain, snow)
- ❑ laundry bag/basket and detergent
- ❑ quarters (lots of them)
- ❑ small drying rack
- ❑ iron/tabletop ironing board (maybe)
- ❑ regular (or extra-long) twin sheets and pillowcases
- ❑ blanket
- ❑ pillow and bedspread or comforter
- ❑ egg-crate mattress pad made out of foam
- ❑ alarm clock/clock radio
- ❑ towels and washcloths
- ❑ shower basket or caddy

- ❏ robe and flip-flops (shower shoes)
- ❏ toiletries of every description
- ❏ hair and makeup stuff—dryer, curling iron, etc.
- ❏ medicine-cabinet items
- ❏ fan and extension cord*
- ❏ desk light
- ❏ 3-prong adapter
- ❏ small tool kit
- ❏ flashlight and batteries
- ❏ duct tape
- ❏ backpack or book bag
- ❏ dictionary/thesaurus
- ❏ calculator, batteries, stapler, ruler
- ❏ desk tray/divider (for neatniks)
- ❏ stamps, stationery, envelopes, postcards (maybe)
- ❏ small calendar planner for assignments
- ❏ message board for outside dorm door
- ❏ cork bulletin board for inside room
- ❏ posters/pictures
- ❏ funtack (gummy adhesive to attach posters and pictures to walls. If you pound nails into the walls or use something that removes paint, you could be fined.)
- ❏ under-bed storage crates/stacking shelves or storage bins, with or without wheels
- ❏ bike and industrial-strength lock
- ❏ beanbag chair
- ❏ carpet/floor mat
- ❏ stereo/boom box/CDs/headphones*

---

* Always check with your school in advance about space and safety regulations before purchasing any appliances.

❑ TV/VCR/DVD player*
❑ answering machine (Check to see if your school offers voice mail.)
❑ camera and film
❑ computer (All colleges have computers. Certain schools may require students to bring their own. If you do bring your own computer, take a 5-plug outlet strip and surge protector with you. See our section on computers.)*
❑ microwave/toaster oven*
❑ mini-refrigerator*
❑ coffeemaker/filters/coffee*
❑ can/bottle opener
❑ dishwashing detergent
❑ plastic plates, bowls, cups
❑ silverware
❑ large bowl for popcorn
❑ chip clips
❑ portable vacuum cleaner
❑ deck of cards/board games
❑ guitar
❑ basketball
❑ Rollerblades
❑ tennis racket
❑ Frisbee
❑ sunscreen
❑ pepper spray

---

* Always check with your school in advance about space and safety regulations before purchasing any appliances.

2.

key items

No matter how much care you take creating your own list of things to bring, there are always surprises. Students said they wish someone had given them a clue about some key items.

TIP!

Anything that is considered important or key is called "clutch," so here's the consensus list of clutch items and some thoughts on a few questionable items as well.

---

closets

> "Bring lots of hangers. I had carefully selected and packed my clothes, and when we got to the dorm room, there was nothing to hang them on."

Since dorms don't provide them, bring the kind of hangers you like. Some students prefer the heft and feel of the plastic tubular hangers. Others say the skinny wire ones are better because you can pack more of them into your closet. Happy campers report that you can unbend the wire hangers and toast marshmallows on them to make s'mores.

Other models include the stacked or cascading hangers that will hold a number of pants or skirts or scarves. There are also hanging deals that have side envelopes or pouches for holding shoes, socks, purses, etc.; they're valuable space savers. It's worth repeating: Room is scarce! Closets are small!

> "I knew our room would have a closet, but didn't know it would have a shelf above the hanging rack. That was great. You need to use every inch of space. I ended up buying some see-through plastic containers to store out-of-season clothes or things I wouldn't be using too often."

fans

Since many dorms are not air-conditioned, nearly everyone brings a fan. Fans are good, because they cool things down.

They also create a steady hum. This pleasant noise blocks out everything so that you can study or sleep.

softer sleep

Many kids found that adding a foam egg-crate mattress pad to a dorm mattress was great for a softer sleep. These can be found in most department and discount stores for a reasonable price. Your college bookstore might carry these, as well.

school supplies

Your campus bookstore will be well stocked with the kinds of notebooks, folders, paper, pens, and desk supplies you'll need. But they are also more expensive. Save money by stocking up on the basics at a discount or office-supply store before you get to campus.

backups

You'll need extra batteries, lightbulbs, printer cartridges, and any unique kind of computer or processor part. These can be a pain to chase down in a strange town, especially if you are on foot and it is raining or snowing and the universe is not coming to greet you and your paper is due tomorrow.

lights

It's helpful to know in advance whether you'll need to bring your own desk light or if one comes with the room. It's essential to have one if you decide to study and your roommate wants to sleep. A computer-science major said she bought a light that she was able to clip to her loft.

> "I don't study in bed, because it's too easy to fall asleep. I enjoy reading just for pleasure at night before I go to sleep. Reading fiction is relaxing after working problem sets."

Another student said that people often end up rearranging their rooms once they know their class schedules and their study habits kick in.

> "Your class schedules, study times, and sleeping habits will often dictate how you will decide to arrange your room."

Another student said that after she went home for Thanksgiving, she brought back a floor lamp and an old chair for reading.

> "I had a survey lit course so I had a ton of reading. It was important to me to have a really comfortable and well-lit place to read in my room."

calendars

You'll need a large wall calendar in your room to write down when major assignments are due. It will help you organize your time. Another good suggestion was to keep a small book-size calendar or Day Runner in your backpack so that you can immediately write down the due dates for papers, lab reports, or major themes.

Or, if you are totally wired, log these dates and times in your PDA (personal digital assistant). Also note the dates of quizzes and tests. You will soon learn that you need to block out study or preparation time and juggle all the other things going on in your life around these key dates.

"One of the biggest surprises to me once I got to college was how few hours you actually spend in class and yet how hectic all the rest of it seems at first. Meeting people, trying to remember names, finding your way to class, remembering to lock your room, going to group information sessions, e-mailing friends, learning when is the best time to eat in the cafeteria on certain days, finding out where you can get a check cashed or use an ATM machine. There's a lot going on. It can all seem overwhelming."

"If you don't organize your time around when key assignments are due and force yourself to plan ahead, you can get way behind and then panic when you suddenly realize the theme or lab report is due tomorrow."

bulletin boards

Essential to help you get organized or tack up tickets, messages, papers, photos—anything you don't want to lose in the general clutter and shuffle of room items.

> ### TIP!
>
> Avoid piles. Get in the habit of putting away clothes, books, papers, laundry, CDs, mail, wet towels, and food. If you take something out, put it back. This will save you time looking for things. It will also cut down on roommate friction.

microwaves

Since they are big energy drainers, check first to see if they are allowed in individual rooms. It may be convenient to have your own, but everyone reports that they are available somewhere in the dorms—in a kitchenette at the end of the hall, in the basement, or at the main desk.

"I just use the microwave in the lounge at the end of the hall. It's convenient and doesn't smell up your room."

tvs

Many students pack a TV. It can be a good escape, free entertainment, or even a quick way to catch up on the news and find out what is happening in the wide world off-campus. One student said she decided to leave hers home next year.

> "It's too easy to get hooked on the soaps or watching reruns of *Law and Order*. You waste time when you should be studying or getting caught up on other things. Besides, all dorms here have TVs in the lounge area, so you can always catch a favorite show or movie. Big sporting events are more fun to watch in a group."

video-game systems

Three students said you should not bring video games, because a) you will spend too much time playing them; and b) you will always have people in your room playing them when you would rather not have them in your room.

vcrs and dvds

These are popular because they can provide entertainment and escape.

"It's a lot cheaper to kick in and rent a video or DVD than it is to go to a show. Disregarding FBI warnings, there is flagrant copying, which leads to lending, swapping, storing schemes, and libraries of every description. However, many dorms have VCRs in their lounge, along with TVs, and show free videos on Friday and Saturday nights."

extra seating

Futons are collapsible couches that come in two parts: frame and mattress. They are great for overnight guests or just to kick back and relax after a long day.

"I got one because I got tired of everyone coming in and sitting on my bed."

Futons come in various sizes and fit well into the corners of most dorm rooms or even under a loft. Futons are expensive—from $100 to $200 new.

TIP!

You might want to wait until spring and get a futon from the senior-hand-me-down circuit. "Seniors sell things for next to nothing or even give things away." Dark colors are best, because of inevitable stains.

lofts

Since dorm rooms are small, many students opt to buy or build lofts, elevated structures for bedding down higher up. Raising your bed off the floor creates prized storage space underneath for your desk, bike, stereo, etc.

> **TIP!**
>
> Check first with your campus housing authority to see if there are restrictions on lofts.

There are usually guidelines stating that lofts cannot block doors, windows, or heating ducts and must allow for x number of inches between the loft and ceiling. Some schools have banned lofts in on-campus housing to prevent students from concocting makeshift structures that can become safety hazards. Many colleges now provide lofts in dorm rooms.

If your school does permit lofts in dormitories and does not provide them for you, you have a couple of options. Many college towns have commercial stores that sell them, so you may be able to purchase one when you arrive on campus. If you'd like to build your own, see the special section we've included in the back of this book (pages 186–95). These instructions will provide you with a sturdy model, provided you use new designated materials, follow the directions, and use it only for sleeping.

back to the books

One student told us his key advice was very simple:

> "Buy a notebook for *each* class. I use a three-ring binder and loose paper. I don't know what I was thinking, except that in high school I had one binder for all my classes. You need a separate one for each course so that you can keep all your homework, tests, quizzes, and papers, plus the syllabus, together with your lecture notes for that class.
>
> "These are really invaluable when it comes time to study for midterms and finals. That way you'll have everything together in one place."

He also said that he now makes a point of writing down each assignment and puts the date on his class notes. "So when a prof says the test will cover all the material since the midterm, you will know where to start studying."

TIP!

Put your name, phone number, and e-mail address in all your notebooks and textbooks, in case you lose them. Also, get the name, phone number, and e-mail address of one person in each class in case you miss a class and need to borrow notes or find out what the next assignment is, etc.

real-life file

Another student said that a key item for her was a large expandable envelope file. She used it to keep her financial aid forms, checks, W-2 forms, allergy and contact lenses prescriptions all in one place—"kind of a real-life file, so I can keep all that stuff together."

freshman handbook

Many colleges publish their own handbook containing information and policies especially designed for first-year students. It's worth checking with the admissions office to see if a comprehensive guide exists. Then again, you may have received one in the mail and just aren't aware of it.

"Of course I was looking forward to college, but once I got my acceptance and my important forms were filled out and mailed in, I quickly lost my enthusiasm. Maybe I was tired of all the paperwork. I wanted to just enjoy my last sweet summer at home. So I must have just quit opening my mail."

"The very first thing I saw when I walked into my dorm was a big welcoming bulletin board. It had everyone's picture, name, and where they were from. Of course mine wasn't up there. It's not that I didn't have thirty leftover senior photos from high school sitting home in my drawer and I couldn't have sent one of them in. So my key tip is a BFO—blinding flash of the obvious: Open all the mail you get from your college, read through it carefully, and respond to it."

In order to get to know students, some people volunteer to work on the dorm social committee. It's a good way to meet people and work on something fun together.

TIP!

If you are more interested in politics than planning parties, consider becoming involved in student government. Nearly all schools have councils, boards, or associations composed of students to deal with issues that affect the student body. You could learn to run your campaign, gain experience in public speaking, and influence people on some aspect of campus life that you care about. Also, it's a good way to meet people with the same kinds of interests and show your commitment to your college.

3.

time management

It's no small task to learn how to get around campus, do your homework, make new friends, find new fun stuff to do, and get your laundry done, too. Many students found managing their time the toughest college assignment of all.

"I really looked forward to being independent and on my own. Then I found out it's hard to be your own boss all the time. There's no one to tell you what to do or when to do it. You have to figure it out yourself and just do it. It's so easy to procrastinate when you have these huge blocks of free time. Then you get down on yourself for wasting valuable time."

"I never thought about the actual freedom that college provides. You make or break yourself. It takes a lot more self-discipline in the beginning to study rather than hang with roommates or friends. Once you become acclimated to each class, studying becomes a little less necessary for some classes and more important for others. You decide what you want out of the class. It's up to you to perform at the level you set your sights on."

———

"Time management is the key to making it through college. Set aside more time to finish assignments than you think you'll need. Take time to study and time to enjoy the social aspects of college. The social aspects are the one thing that brings most students down. However, if you manage your time successfully, you will be amazed at how much free time you actually have."

———

"Stay fluid. Work the balance: mind • heart • body • soul."

———

"The whole key is to get in the habit of being organized and not putting things off until the last minute. A lot of that is forcing yourself to sit down and study and do laundry when you don't feel like it."

———

"College is about so many things going on at the same time. Everything seems so random. I'd advise freshmen to try to get into a pattern early, develop a schedule or routine for each day. That helps a lot."

making choices

New situations often provide new opportunities for establishing new priorities.

"There are so many new things to do and get involved in. I came here to run track. We ran twenty hours a week. What I found out was, track, for me, wasn't about the love of the sport. What I really liked about it was winning. In order to do that at college, to make it to the top, the cost seemed too high. What if I spent the next three years running twenty hours a week and never won another race? I would be disappointed, spending that much time trying to do that when there was so much else here to do. So I quit after my first year. The news wasn't real well received at home. But it was the right choice for me."

"I was on the volleyball team my first two years at school. It was a lot of hard work and a lot of fun. But my junior year, I decided I was more interested in getting involved in leadership opportunities in my fraternity and other campus activities that would help me later in my career. I'm glad now I chose to do those other things."

"Yes, it's huge, the daily time commitment you make. This is my senior year and I'm doing my student teaching. After teaching all day, I go to the gym for basketball practice. We practice three and a half hours. Why do I do it? I just love to play basketball.

Plus, some of my best friends are on the team. We have a great time."

"Sports were always a big part of my high school life. I was thrilled to receive a volleyball scholarship. I made my best grades during volleyball season when the team was traveling. So sometimes a full schedule can force you to get more done than an open one."

balancing act

So what is the secret to acquiring good time-management skills? Students agreed the key was to keep track of things by writing them down or logging them into an electronic calendar device. This means listing classes, assignments, study time, and all the other things that make up your day.

If you are a free spirit who loves an unstructured life, this may seem hard, or at the very least insanely tedious. But it does work. To help you get into this process, we've included the daily time planner that follows. Feel free to photocopy or scan this form.

Take a look at it and imagine filling in the time squares based on your senior year. Mentally log in the time you spent in class every day. What activities did you do after school? Sports, yearbook, band, drama, part-time work, volunteer, hang out, watch TV, surf the Internet, talk on the phone? Did you have any chores at home you were expected to do on a regular basis?

Now log in your current schedule of classes. In high school it might have been from 8:30 to 3:30 every day, or thirty-five hours per week. A normal college load would be fifteen or sixteen class hours a week. Your first class may start at 8 A.M; then your next class may be at 6 P.M. Or you may have three hours of class five days a week, with all morning or all afternoon free.

That's why juggling your time is harder in college: There's more free time to juggle and more spaces in between. So what do you do when you are not in class? Hopefully, you'll study, eat, sleep, play, and take care of routine maintenance.

breaking things down

When it comes to class assignments, the key tip is to break down the large ones into small bite-size pieces. If you are taking a survey course that requires reading a book or two per week, scope it out. Do the math. Add up the chapters you need to cover and divide by five. Then block out the time it will take to read them over the course of a week. Be specific. Instead of filling in "Monday 2–5, Lit," write "Monday 2–5, Lit, read chapters 1–12."

Think back to when you had to write your first long paper or report in middle school. What were the steps the teacher outlined? They probably looked something like this:

1. Select a topic.
2. Decide how you will gather information—on the Internet, in the library, from magazines, interviewing people?
3. Do the research.
4. Prepare an outline.
5. Write a rough draft.

6. Review (or have teacher review) and revise.
7. Complete final version of report.

Your teacher might have tried to motivate you by saying something like "Every journey of a thousand miles begins with a single step." It's very easy to put off doing something new or hard. The longer you delay getting started, the harder it becomes to take the first step.

> "If I'd spend half the time studying that I think
> about studying or worrying about not getting it right,
> I'd be home free."

Application

Try applying this step-by-step technique to other things you don't especially enjoy doing. Figure out approximately how long it will take to perform certain tasks. Then you can mentally click and drag something from an emotional dread zone to a more neutral time zone. By doing this you change your focus from the dreaded activity itself to the objective time it takes to do it.

I do not get a kick out of walking to my eight o'clock class when it is 5 degrees out, balancing my checking account, or doing my laundry. However, if you tell yourself this will take just twenty or thirty or sixty minutes and it will be over and done with, it may become easier to do.

Room Detail

Here's what to do when you find out that parents' weekend is coming up and your room is a pit. (This is for my nephew, when he was a freshman at Indiana University. Matt has a warm and happy heart and splendid mind. However, rumor has it that his room is on the verge of being declared a dorm disaster area.)

- Pick up any loose or dried-up food—half-eaten taco, stray popcorn, slice of pizza with all the pepperoni picked off, mashed gummy bears, etc. Check on floor, under bed or loft, and between futon and mattress.
- Throw above items into the trash.
- If you spot anything dark and moving while doing this, squash it. Remove dead object with a piece of toilet paper.
- Pick up any disposable containers—cans, bottles, plastic cups, lids, straws, bags, and cartons.
- Gather up books, notebooks, important papers. Pick up old magazines, newspapers, flyers—read or pitch.
- Take trash to wherever you dispose of trash.
- Put all CDs, DVDs, and videos back into their respective jackets or racks.
- Pick up shoes, caps, and sporting gear and put in closet. Pick up all clothes, socks, towels, and underwear lying on the floor and deposit in laundry basket, bag, or bin.
- Make bed.
- Before you go down to do your laundry, take an already dirty towel and eliminate obvious dust mites and mop up any spilled liquids.
- Extra Credit: Go down to the front desk. Leave I.D. card and return with communal vacuum

cleaner. Vacuum room. Return vacuum cleaner to
desk. Don't forget your I.D. card. Return to clean
room. Take picture. Send photo out via the Web.

Learning Curve

It will take time to figure out what you need to do on a daily
and weekly basis. Primarily, your day will be organized
around your class times. You may not have a great deal of
choice in selecting when you want to take a certain class
your first year. However, by trial and error you should be
able to discover the kind of schedule that works best for you.

Some people learn and think best in the morning. Others
brighten up in the afternoon. One thing most students find
is that it is easier to develop better study habits if they have
extended free time periods rather than having short periods
between classes throughout the day.

> "It's too easy to waste time if you have an hour or two
> between classes. You don't really get much accom-
> plished."

academic advice

In addition to formulating a class time/study time schedule,
you will also need to think about the kinds of courses to take.
Your A.A. (academic adviser) or F.A. (faculty adviser) will
help you with that. We asked a professor who has spent years
counseling freshmen what advice he would offer. This is
what he said:

"Here's what I know from experience. The first semester of the freshman year is always the toughest, for almost everyone. Normally the GPA for the first semester will be lower than those that follow. The reasons are obvious: There is a new environment to adapt to, and college is harder than high school. I thought I was pretty good coming out of high school but made mostly C's in courses my first year.

"I see many freshmen wanting to do everything their first semester or year. They are eager to get their required courses out of the way. They will want to take a heavy reading course, freshmen comp, math, a foreign language, and other tough classes like computer science and econ. To take on too much of a load your first term can be a recipe for disaster.

"I advise them to cut themselves some slack. Take an elective that really interests them or get a PE class out of the way. Get adjusted to campus life, college professors, and college-level courses first."

Courses and Majors

When asked about the kinds of classes for first-year students and the "major" question, the professor expressed the following views:

"I think survey courses have taken a bum rap. We have many of our best teachers in those freshman courses, because they are a good way for them to recruit majors to their field. While small seminars, which provide for a lot of student discussion, receive a great deal of attention these days, I think there is still a place for the lecture course. Students need the experience of hearing ideas presented, processing them, and beginning to learn how to ask the right questions.

"I tell students not to worry if they haven't selected a major. They may discover a subject or field they get excited about during their first two years [that] they didn't even know existed. Also, our school, like many other colleges, doesn't require you to declare a major until the end of your sophomore year.

"Finally, I tell students to realize that this is not the real world. I encourage them to get outside the college bubble. Stay connected to the outside world. Watch CNN. Read a newspaper. There's a lot going on out there while you are here inside the bubble. This will help them put their college experience into a broader perspective."

Daily Time Planner
For the Week of _____

	Monday	Tuesday	Wednesday	Thursday	Friday	Saturday	Sunday
8:00							
9:00							
10:00							
11:00							
NOON							
1:00							
2:00							

continued on next page . . .

	Monday	Tuesday	Wednesday	Thursday	Friday	Saturday	Sunday
3:00							
4:00							
5:00							
6:00							
7:00							
8:00							
9:00							
10:00							
11:00							
12:00							

4.

health care hints

Getting sick is always a major downer. It can seem worse if you are away from home for the first time and have to cope on your own, and it is huge if you come down with the flu in the middle of major projects or exams. We interviewed a physician, personnel at a campus health center, and several pharmacists to see what advice they had for new college students. Here's what we found.

A doctor who had two daughters in college gave this key piece of advice:

"The body works best when it is on a regular routine. It's important to establish good health habits and patterns early. Try to build a regular schedule around classes, studying, eating, sleeping, and exercising."

He added that it was especially important to get enough
sleep:

> **"Even missing one night's sleep wears down the
> immune system and lowers your resistance to any
> bug or virus. Students who routinely pull all-
> nighters end up paying for it. The brain simply
> doesn't function as well if it has been up for eigh-
> teen to twenty-four hours straight. Ask any doctor
> doing a residency who has been on duty for
> twenty or thirty hours how he or she is doing.
> They will verify this."**

You probably haven't given any thought to trying to stay
healthy at college. You should. Why?

> **"It's just easier to catch things. Students are usu-
> ally sharing common rest rooms. Sleeping quar-
> ters are often tight, with poor ventilation. Because
> of the number of people living in crowded quar-
> ters, viruses can spread more rapidly."**

immunization history

> **"Most colleges require freshmen to submit a
> health-screening history or a record of immu-
> nizations they have received. Some, like tetanus,
> may need to be renewed. Two vaccines, for hepati-
> tis B and meningitis, may be listed as optional. I
> recommend students receive them. The meningo-**

coccal virus [meningitis] moves through the body very rapidly, with devastating—often deadly—results. I believe in the ounce-of-prevention-is-worth-a-pound-of-cure adage."

TIP!

Both the American College Health Association and the Centers for Disease Control recommend that college freshmen be vaccinated for hepatitis B and meningitis. To check out the ACHA guideline recommendations for immunizations, see *http://www.acha. org* or contact your campus health center.

---

campus health centers

We asked a nurse at a campus health center if the clinic carries the vaccines for hepatitis B and meningitis.

"Yes, if freshmen are not able to get them at home, we carry them here. Menomume, the meningitis vaccine, costs $70 and is needed only once. By the age of twenty-five, most people have built up immunity."

We asked her what kinds of symptoms she most commonly sees.

"Colds and flu are the most common. It takes just one person to come down with a cold or case of the flu. Soon we end up treating the whole house [sorority or fraternity] or dorm. I tell them all the common-sense rules really apply.

"Washing hands is the number-one way to prevent germs from spreading. It doesn't have to be antibacterial soap. Any soap will do. I tell them to sing the alphabet song while they wash with hot water and soap. When they're done with the song, their hands are clean.

[You may want to just sing this inside your head if there are other people around.]

"If roommates are sharing a computer in their room and one has a cold or flu, the other should wash his or her hands or use a waterless hand sanitizer before using the mouse. Germs spread on surfaces. Another obvious way to prevent spreading germs is to cover your mouth when you sneeze or cough, and avoid people who don't.

"Sometimes students come in and tell us they feel very tired and are afraid they might have mono. Usually, mononucleosis starts out with symptoms much like strep throat—sore throat, swollen glands, etc. It's sometimes known as 'the kissing disease,' but more likely the virus is picked up when students are run-down, sleep-deprived, or have poor eating habits. Diets high in fat lower the immune system."

What are some other things you would like freshmen to know?

"Students should know that when they come to the health center, the care or treatment they receive is confidential. We do not share information without their signing a written consent form. In the fall, members of our medical staff make evening presentations in the dorms and sororities and fraternities on alcohol awareness, date rape, sexually transmitted diseases, depression, and eating disorders. We encourage students to come to the health center immediately if they are dealing with any of these problems."

be prepared

Are there any medicine-chest items students should bring with them?

"I'd suggest students bring a digital thermometer. We often get calls from kids saying they think they have a fever. If they can take their own temperature and then call us, that would be very helpful.

"I also recommend they stop by and get a flu shot. We begin making the vaccine available in October.

"Bring some basic items with you, such as an Ace bandage for sprains. Bring extra safety pins, as the little metal clips wear out. Also, we recom-

mend instant ice packs for bruises and swelling. Since students have access to refrigerators but usually not freezers, these work well and are easy to keep on a shelf until needed."

Many of the students we talked to had packed some common medical-cabinet supplies and taken them to school in a shoe box. Students recommended a variety of popular items.

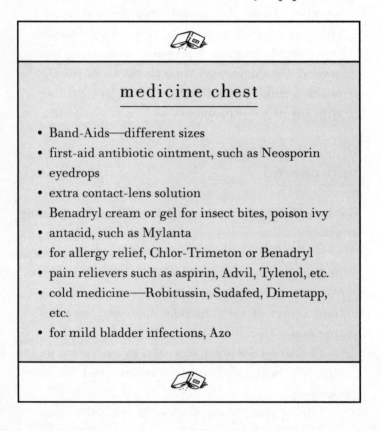

medicine chest

- Band-Aids—different sizes
- first-aid antibiotic ointment, such as Neosporin
- eyedrops
- extra contact-lens solution
- Benadryl cream or gel for insect bites, poison ivy
- antacid, such as Mylanta
- for allergy relief, Chlor-Trimeton or Benadryl
- pain relievers such as aspirin, Advil, Tylenol, etc.
- cold medicine—Robitussin, Sudafed, Dimetapp, etc.
- for mild bladder infections, Azo

prescription drugs

If you are on any prescription drugs, obviously you'll want to take them with you. If you run out while you are at school, you can call your doctor's office or health care clinic at home. Many have a twenty-four-hour line for prescription refills that is checked several times a day. You should know:

- name and dosage of drug
- doctor's phone number or home drugstore number
- campus pharmacy number

Give them the name and phone number of the campus pharmacy or drugstore where you want to pick up the drug. Calling your doctor's office is the first thing to do. However, some pharmacies will call the doctor for you so that you can get your prescription filled. It's worth a try if you are trying to speed up the process.

Out-of-State Prescriptions

If you are going to a school in your home state, you should not have to be concerned about getting your prescriptions filled. However, if you are going to school in California and live out of state, you need to know that California does not accept prescriptions written by an out-of-state physician. You may need to call someone at home and have him or her mail you your prescription, or ask the doctor at your school's health center to write the prescription for you. Or you might consider ordering your prescription online from a reliable website.

insurance or hmo card

If you are covered by a parent's health-insurance plan, get a card of your own and carry it with you. If no cards for dependents are available, you will need to have this information:

- insurance company or HMO
- policy number
- blood type
- allergies
- doctor's phone number
- parents' phone number

If you visit your campus health care center, give them a copy of this information for your file. Advise them of any medication or special care you are receiving. A lab technician we spoke to said,

"Some of our students are on Accutane, and require a monthly blood test. We can do that here and fax the results to their doctor at home. We try to do everything we can to ensure continuity of care with the student's personal physician. Students who are being treated for diabetes, thyroid problems, etc., need to be aware of this."

> ### TIP!
>
> If you are visiting your health care center on campus during heavy cold or flu periods, you may have to wait. Take a book along. Some centers have adjoining pharmacies, where you may be able to get prescriptions filled more cheaply than in off-campus drugstores. If you are out of cash, ask if they will put the charge on your bursar's bill. Some will.

drug news

While you may think of pharmacists as people who count pills and measure potions, they are really the drug experts. To become one, you must have five or six years of college, depending on the state licensing, and have taken about forty hours of chemistry. One pharmacist told us: "Usually, we are busy trying to get patients', doctors', and hospitals' prescriptions filled. I miss being able to use more of the knowledge I spent years learning. I'm glad when I have time to answer questions about recommendations or about how a drug may interact with something a customer is already taking. Students may find it useful to know that the following medicines are now available without a prescription:

- L-Lysine—for cold sores, fever blisters
- Zantac—for nervous stomach; relieves acid indigestion
- Tavist—an antihistamine that does not produce

drowsiness. For allergy symptoms—runny nose, itchy eyes, sneezing

- Imodium—for diarrhea and abdominal cramping"

TIP!

- Take a daily vitamin.
- Take extra vitamin C during cold season.
- Take B vitamins for jumpy nerves.
- Use sunscreen, summer and winter.
- Drink a quart of water every day.
- Don't live on just coffee, Coke, and beer.
- Eat as many raw fruits and vegetables as possible.
- Take Emetrol for nausea.
- Zinc lozenges and vitamin C provide good relief for sore throats.
- Listerine strips are great for stopping coughs.
- Replace toothbrushes after you've had the flu or a cold.
- Stay away from diet pills, especially those with Ephedra and mahuang. They can be dangerous and may cause serious health problems. A proper diet combined with regular exercise is more effective and much safer.
- Try vitamin E for menstrual cramping and heavy flow. Take 400 IU daily.
- Use store brands of vitamins or medicines to save money. Most are just as effective and much cheaper.

glasses and contacts

If you wear glasses or contacts, you may want to get a copy of your prescription before you leave for school. Also, check with your vision center to see how you can most quickly replace lost contacts. If you wear disposable lenses, purchase new ones before you get down to your last pair.

TRUE STORY

Several students interviewed said they preferred to go to a local hospital for X rays, stitches, or broken bones. Their parents reported learning about these incidents only when they received the bill from the hospital or lab. Mothers especially find this kind of mail upsetting. So phone home and clue them in on any accidents or emergency visits to the hospital. If nothing else, it will give them something specific to worry about.

5.

safety advice

Colleges are not safe havens from the real world of home-land security. Whether your campus is in a rural or urban setting, you need to be smart about protecting yourself and your belongings. You must learn to be watchful and live defensively. Here is good advice from students at both private schools and large universities.

locking your room

Although R.A.s (resident assistants) will tell students to lock their rooms at all times, whether you do or not depends on a number of factors, including the size of your dorm and what floor you live on.

"If you live on the first or second floor, you will see a lot of through and random traffic. I'd say it is better always to lock up on these floors, especially on weekends when there is something major going on, like a football game. There can be lots of visitors roaming the halls. The upper floors, where many kids have single rooms, are much more remote and quiet."

One student told us that he and his roommate always locked their door at first, but after getting to know the other guys on the floor better, felt okay with locking it only when they went down to the cafeteria or left the building.

"The last one in always locks the door at night. We're on the twelfth floor, so we don't lock the windows, but those living on the ground floors do so at night."

A young woman said that when she or her roommate left their room just to go to the bathroom or to talk to someone down the hall, they generally just left the door open. Others told us they always locked their door, even if they were just going to take a shower.

"My roommate and I both lost our keys the first week of school and just kept our door closed rather than taking the time to get new keys. We never got them and never had anything stolen. I'm not sure if I'd recommend this or not. We were just lucky."

theft control

Here's the scoop:

- Bikes and cars should be locked at all times. Avoid leaving or parking these in isolated areas. Always lock your bike *to* something else.
- If you have real jewelry, wear it or hide it.
- Be careful where you put small items—cell phones, calculators, cameras, Walkmans, watches, CDs, sunglasses, Palm Pilots.
- Never leave your backpack or a laptop anywhere.
- When you go home for holidays or spring break, lock your bike in your room and take any expensive items home with you.
- Check your parents' homeowners'/rental policy to see if your property will be covered at college. One agent told us: "Most insurance companies provide some personal-property coverage at a secondary residence. It's always a good idea to check with your agent to see if you have additional coverage. Some policies may require a rider for computers."

personal precautions

Guys didn't seem to feel uneasy walking or running around campus in the evening or early morning hours. Most of the girls did. Here are some of their suggestions:

- Take well-lighted paths at night. Avoid the shortcuts you might take during the day.
- Make it a point to be with someone, whether this means finding an early-morning or late-evening jogging partner. Don't be afraid to ask someone to walk back with you after a late class or an after-hours function.
- Take a martial arts class as one of your phys ed courses.

"I took karate and got an A+. I could use it if I had to defend myself."

- Carry pepper spray.

"I haven't had to use it, but it makes me feel more secure to have it on my key chain in case I am attacked."

campus safety

Every college in the country wants to provide a safe environment for its students. Be prepared to have fire drills in your dorm, to receive special warnings via e-mail, to hear sirens for practice evacuation drills, or to hear megaphone announcements about weather and safety alerts.

"I was going out of my dorm my first month at school. Then I saw R.A.s were on bullhorns telling everyone to get to the basement of the dorm. A tornado had touched down ten miles from campus."

Escort Service

In addition to the basic safety precautions and procedures mentioned above, all the students we talked to said that their schools had some type of security escort service that was free.

On a large campus you can call a SAFE number and tell the operator where you are and a bus will pick you up in about ten minutes and deliver you to your residence. A small campus may have a SAFE RIDE van that makes regular stops in the evening. A SAFE call in California might mean that someone will come by and pick you up in a golf cart. SAFE vehicles are easily identifiable, and people driving them usually wear a vest or jacket to identify themselves. These vehicles may also be called to pick up and take students back to their residence if they are too drunk to drive or walk home.

TRUE STORY

One female student who worked late at night learned that if you are walking by yourself and see a stranger approaching, it is important to make eye contact with him and yet at the same time not try to stare him down.

"If you look down and avoid his eyes, you'll look like you are afraid and appear vulnerable." Another thing she does is that although she doesn't smoke, she often carries a lit cigarette when she is walking home late at night to make her appear more tough or independent.

6.

transportation tips: cars, bikes, planes, buses, and blades

Many colleges do not allow freshmen to bring cars. Some will issue a permit if there are special circumstances that make it necessary for you to have one. If you do bring a car, you may end up having to park in a designated lot a long way from your residence hall, sorority, or fraternity. Bottom line: Do you really need a car? Do you need the expense or the responsibility?

car talk

If you do take a car to campus, here are some key tips:

- Buy a campus permit for your car right away. One freshman who brought her car said she got her permit right away but was issued a ticket for parking illegally the first week. "I'm appealing it.

I didn't even know it was a no-parking space." She also received a speeding ticket, which cost her a cool $100.

"I put off getting one, because I was trying to get settled in my room and figure out my class schedule. I ended up getting my permit a week after I had been on campus. The fine was steep—$30 per day."

- Always lock your car. Buy a hide-a-key for the door key. Hide an extra ignition key somewhere inside your car. If you have a newer-model car with one key for everything, make two copies of it and hide one outside and one inside.
- Find a local mechanic you can trust by asking someone who lives in the town—the janitor in your dorm or a secretary or your R.A.—for a recommendation. When you take your car in, describe the problem you've been having. Ask what could be wrong and how much it will cost to fix it. Instruct the mechanic to call you first if he finds the repair is going to cost more than the original estimate.

"The worst thing is to just leave your car and say fix it and then get stuck with a big bill. You don't know whether it is legitimate or not. Another suggestion— always save car bills."

Loaning Out

Should you loan out your car?

> "Some people you know you can trust, others you just wouldn't. Whatever decision you make, lay out some ground rules or conditions ahead of time, like no drinking, the time you will need your car returned, etc."

TRUE STORY

One student borrowed a car to visit his girlfriend at another school. He had an accident on the way home. The good news—he wasn't hurt. The bad news—neither his insurance nor that of the car owner covered the damage, which was extensive.

Moral: If you loan out your car to people, make sure their insurance covers them while they are driving your car.

Just Like Mom

Realize that you could potentially end up being a full-time chauffeur.

> "If I'm on my way somewhere or going to be making a run in the same direction, I don't mind giving someone a ride. On the other hand, taking kids to the airport before holidays or picking them up when they get back can get old in a hurry."

TIP!

Many colleges or universities located in small towns or cities have a shuttle bus to the nearest airport that runs several times a day. You should be able to find the schedule on the school's website. If your school provides this service, suggest this as a friendly alternative to a friend who is begging a ride.

Reasonable Returns

If you borrow someone else's car, especially for a road trip, return it in good shape. Fill it up with gas, clean the windows, and get rid of any cartons, wrappers, cans, or bottles before you return the car.

Essentials

Sometimes bad things happen, even to good drivers. So have this info handy:

- ❏ insurance company and phone number
- ❏ policy number
- ❏ driver's license number
- ❏ license plate number
- ❏ on-campus permit number

> **TIP!**
>
> Have your car and tires thoroughly checked and ser-
> viced before you leave for campus. Put jumper cables
> and a flashlight in the trunk.

Don't drive and talk on your cell phone at the same time.
It might even be illegal in the state where your school is located. Watch out for bikes.

bikes

Bikes abound on all campuses. They are good because they
do not require gas or expensive insurance.

"Bikes are great to get there quicker. Like when you
have a paper due in five minutes in a hall fifteen
blocks away. You can make it on time and not have to
worry about finding a place to park."

Night Riders

In addition to serving a functional role as transportation,
bikes are also recreational stress busters.

"Sometimes a bunch of guys in the dorm will get
late-night bursts of energy. We get on our bikes and
break away from the books for midnight stealth rides
downtown—a great escape and mood booster."

> ### TIP!
>
> Always lock your bike to something else—a bike rack, pole, etc.

TRUE STORY

Don't bring or buy an expensive bike, but do buy an expensive U-type lock and use it. One student bought a $275 bike and a Kryptonite lock. He ran into some friends, hung out with them for a couple of hours, and returned to find that someone had totally lifted the bike and lock. He had a part-time job delivering documents from the chemical engineering department to other buildings on campus. His boss, feeling sorry for him after hearing that he'd had his new bike stolen, gave him her old bike.

"It was so trashy-looking I didn't think anyone would want it. Still, I would lock it up—until one time when I was in a hurry to deliver the documents on time and didn't bother. When I returned five minutes later, the bike was gone. As if to taunt me, the thief left the lock on the ground where the bike had been."

Moral: Do not bring an expensive bike to college. Do buy a Kryptonite lock and use it. Don't leave your bike alone for long periods of time. Lock it in your room before you go home for the holidays.

planes

If you fly to and from school, be sure to make your reservations for Thanksgiving or Christmas three months in advance. A couple of weeks before, call the airline to see if it is still in business and to confirm your seat and departure time. Sometimes airlines will schedule extra flights during peak travel periods, which could change the departure time or your flight number or both. Consider sticking with one airline in order to accumulate frequent-flyer miles.

Reality Check

If your parents are going to meet your flight, tell them the airline, flight number, and estimated time of arrival. Tell them to call and check to see if your plane is running on time before they leave home to pick you up. Flights have been known to run late. This could save your loved ones from having to hang around the airport for a long time waiting for your plane to come in.

TIP!

Be sure to allow yourself plenty of time to get to the airport and go through the security check. Have a means of identification with your picture on it—your driver's license or your student I.D. International students will need their passports.

Keep Your Ears Open and Hands Clean

Flying while you have a head cold or ear infection can be painful. Some flight attendants suggest taking a decongestant to try to keep your ears open, or chewing lots of gum. Do your best to avoid spreading your cold—or to pick up one from someone else. Because of the limited air supply in packed cabins, germs spread quickly and easily. Wash your hands when possible, or consider using a waterless hand-cleaning product like Purell. Products like these are all available in small travel-size containers.

Hang On to Your Ticket

If your plans change and you are not able to use a ticket when you planned, call the airline's reservations department and let them know right away. Many airlines will void tickets if you skip your flight or fail to notify them in advance. Their policies differ on how long they will honor a ticket or let you rebook a flight—anywhere from six months to a year. Usually, there is a charge for rewriting the ticket unless you can offer proof of death (someone else's) or illness, in which case the fee may be waived. If you buy a round-trip ticket and will not be using the return ticket, check to see what the airline might give you for it.

Electronic Ticketing

If you have a paper ticket and lose it, you are out of luck. For this reason, many students use electronic ticketing. Your name is entered into the airline's computer system when you book your ticket. When you check in for your flight, all

you have to do is give your name and provide proper identification. If you booked your trip through a travel service,
show the printed itinerary you were given. If you did the
booking yourself and bought your ticket online, be sure to
print out your itinerary. For security reasons, almost all airlines will want to see your printed itinerary before they permit you to board the plane.

Lost and Found

All airlines have lost-and-found departments. If you get
home and discover you've left something on the plane, call
the airport where you landed and report it. If the flight continued after you got off, you may want to call the lost-and-
found department in the city of the plane's final destination.
Cleaners have been known to discover all kinds of items
while servicing planes.

TIP!

Tag all items with your name, permanent home address, phone number, and e-mail address. Do this
both for baggage you check and for items you take on
board with you.

Extra Fees

Be prepared to pay additional fees if you exceed the number
of bags you are allowed to check. Fees may also be added for
oversize bags or boxes.

Overbooked Flights

If the flight you planned to take is overbooked, the ticket agent may announce a free ticket to passengers who are willing to give up their seats and take a later flight. If you aren't too eager to get home or return to campus, this can be a very good deal. Often, the next flight will mean only a few hours' wait—and you'll have a free ticket!

buses

Many campuses have buses that transport people around campus. These are very handy if the weather is bad or you're tired. Check out the routes in advance. Monthly or semester passes are very inexpensive.

Escape Routes

Buses can also provide you with an opportunity to escape campus life for a while, whether your destination is a nearby shopping mall or another city.

> "We have a bus that runs to the city on a couple of Saturdays in November and December, in case you want to go Christmas shopping or check out the bright lights."

> "I find it is vital for my sanity to just get off campus and away from everyone once a month. Buses are cheap and a great escape."

blades

Some students get from class to class on Rollerblades. This means of transport is not for the weak or timid.

7.

clothes and laundry

While campus styles and fashion statements may vary, jeans, sweats, T-shirts, shorts, sneakers, and sandals are the universal college uniform—regardless of labels or price tags. Pack these basics and you'll look at home anywhere.

clothes

The general consensus is to take fewer clothes to school with you rather than more. One guy told us, "Don't take too much. I brought my heavy coat with me in August. It took up so much room in my closet I ended up bringing it back home until I needed it—three months later."

"At first you think you need a ton of clothes. But you end up wearing things that you like and that are easy to take care of. I ended up taking about half the clothes I brought with me back home."

———

"The closet and drawer space are really limited; you don't have room for everything you'd like to take. I'd suggest taking just the clothes you really like."

Styles and Options

As far as what kinds of clothes to take with you, the best tip is to check out what people are wearing when you first visit the campus. Looks, styles, or statements may vary according to schools or climates. A woman professor who has taught at four different colleges said she found that different campuses tend to go for different looks—from Gap to Polo to Bean. "It's interesting to me that each year there always seems to be one or two accessories almost everyone seems to latch on to. Also, wearing a lot of black is still popular."

TIP!

"While you'll want to pack a lot of the basics, you may want to wait and purchase some optional gear once you are on campus. I didn't buy everything before I went. I saved some of my money that I had budgeted for clothes and bought some special things after I saw what other kids were wearing."

> **TIP!**
>
> "You don't need to dress up for class. My best ad-vice—comfortable shoes are a must! There can be a lot of walking in the rain."

From Preppy to Grunge-du-Jour

"I'd say girls seem to pay more attention to what they wear than guys. I was surprised how many girls here wear skirts to class, along with taking prep time with hair and makeup. I went to a private girls' school. It was pleated skirts and white blouses for four years. I love being able to wear jeans to class and to push my hair up under a baseball cap."

Indian Summers

Remember that it can still be hot in September and October in many places in the country, so bring enough lightweight clothing. On many campuses you can get by with a couple of sweaters, jeans, and a light jacket long into fall.

"At first you think you need to take everything with you that you'll ever need for your entire freshman year. Then you learn that you pack some things, take them home at Thanksgiving, and then take wintery things back to campus."

Shop or Swap

Girls tend to swap or borrow clothes more than guys. It's okay as long as it doesn't bother you. If you are an only child, it may seem weird to trade or borrow.

It's also okay to say no nicely. One suggestion on how to handle it: "I'm glad you like my hand-knit sweater, but I don't want to get in the habit of loaning things out." You don't have to apologize or explain, as people tend to take you at your word. However, it's a good idea to make up your mind one way or the other and then stick to your decision.

TIP!

"One piece of advice I'd pass on is that you never want to just raid someone's closet and borrow something without asking. That can cause major flare-ups! I don't mind if someone needs something generic of mine for a skit or something, like a black turtleneck or white blouse or sweatshirt. But I don't loan out my other things."

Returns

If you do loan out your clothes, tell the loanee how you want the item returned—if you want it washed, hung, dryer-dried, or dry-cleaned. One student said, "I learned this the hard way when someone returned something of mine they had washed and dried and it had shrunk."

Which leads right into another popular subject that produced prodigious responses.

laundry

Universal clutch recommendation:

> "Watch out for *hot* dryers. They can turn your stuff into doll clothes. Make a test run on sheets or towels first so you can see how hot the dryers are."

To Iron or Not to Iron

Some students iron shirts or blouses and press items for special occasions. Others said they don't bother.

"I just make sure I pull my clothes out of the dryer and hang them up right away."

One guy claimed he was ironing-impaired. "I never iron anything." He appeared rumply but happy.

We asked another student if anyone ever irons. "There's an ironing board down at the end of the hall in the kitchenette. I think the only time it is really used is in the spring, when there is a job fair on campus and everyone wants to look their best. Lots of guys get haircuts then, too."

Basic Laundry List

- Separate white or light clothes from dark ones.
- Check the labels to see if you should wash items in cold or warm water.
- Empty your pockets before you put things in the washer.
- Wash any red or bright pink clothes, especially

sweats, by themselves to avoid having clothes that
all have a monotone pinkish glow.

There are always exceptions:

"Everyone says to read the labels first, but I don't
have time for that. I just wash everything in cold
water and most of my stuff turns out fine."

TIP!

Don't try to do your laundry on weekends, when
everyone else does. Off times during the week are
best.

"I do my wash every Wednesday morning at two A.M.
No problem. It's automatic, just like going to a class."

Take a stash of quarters with you so you don't have to go
around begging for change in the wee small hours of the
morning.

"I keep a cup of quarters hidden in the bottom of my
laundry bag so they are always there where I need
them."

Theft Control

Some students report you need to stay with your laundry so that it doesn't get stolen, dumped on top of the dryer, or dumped on the floor.

> "I always do something while I'm waiting in the laundry room—read a magazine, write postcards, do my nails—so it's not so bad. I try to think of it as a break rather than a chore."

Another student starts his laundry and then goes up to his room. There, he sets a kitchen timer to go off when the cycle is finished. At the sound of the buzzer, he returns for his laundry.

Drying Time

If your things are just partially dry and you don't have time to wait around for them, you can take them up to your room and put them on a small drying rack. A couple kids said these racks are a must.

> "I didn't bring one along and so I just staggered my chest of drawers and formed a makeshift rack of my own until I could buy one."

Another student says she uses her drying rack for T-shirts and her part-spandex clothes so that they don't shrink.

Bounce It Out

Almost everyone runs into the scrunch problem: You want to wear a certain item, but it isn't clean and you don't have time to wash it. You can put the item in a dryer with a sheet of fabric softener for five or ten minutes to freshen it up.

But be forewarned:

"It's not a good idea to overdo this technique unless you want to become a kind of walking ad for Bounce."

TRUE STORY

Try to do your laundry on a regular basis. One freshman had trouble getting around to it. He returned to his fraternity house one lovely Friday afternoon in the fall. When he got ready to take a shower, he discovered that his fraternity brothers had buried all his towels in the backyard.

Laundromat Option

One student said she got tired of always having to wait around for a washer to be free and then wait again for a free dryer:

"I ended up finding it was easier to take my clothes to a large laundromat on campus. There are always plenty of machines. That way you can get it all done and over with at once. Also, sometimes laundromats are a good place to meet people—or get away from the dorm for a while."

8.

food
and exercise
and sleep

Most students have gotten the message on the mind-body connection. They make a real effort to eat right and get daily exercise—to stay in shape and relieve stress. Many identified getting enough sleep as a real problem. When asked what he will do differently his sophomore year, one student replied, "Next year I'll bring more underwear, eat better, and get some sleep."

food

Meal Plans
Most of the students we spoke to reported that the food at college was pretty average—not dreadful, but not exactly great. Typically, students sign up for a meal plan in which

they make advance payment for ten to twenty meals a week. One coed said that at her college, in order to encourage first-year students to adopt regular and healthy eating habits, they must sign up for a minimum of fifteen meals a week for their first year. "There's a month's worth of meals embedded in your magnetic meal card. You just swipe it through the machine and get in line."

Point Systems

On other campuses, students purchase "points," which they may use in cafeterias, snack shops, or even a McDonald's that is housed in the basement of a dorm.

> "We have a convenience store in the basement of our dorm. You can use your points to buy microwave meals. They also sell cake mixes, which is neat. Sometimes my friends and I buy them and make one when someone has a birthday."

One student, who frequently goes home on weekends and so does not need her food points, uses her points to purchase other items the store carries—soap, laundry detergent, and tissues.

Credit-Access Cards

One freshman reported that his student I.D. serves as his meal card and can also be used as a credit-access card. There are machines on campus where you put in your card and insert a twenty-dollar bill (or ten or fifty dollars—whatever amount you think you'll need), and then your card is embedded with twenty dollars of credit. That way you can use it at off-campus locations that are on the credit-access-card (CAC) system.

"I carry my CAC and leave my billfold at home. It's safer than carrying cash. It would be hard for someone else to use my card, since it has my picture on it."

Back to the Room

Ordering out for pizza or making the ever-popular border run (Taco Bell) can get expensive in a hurry. Since class schedules vary widely and many students participate in extracurricular activities, most people keep food in their rooms.

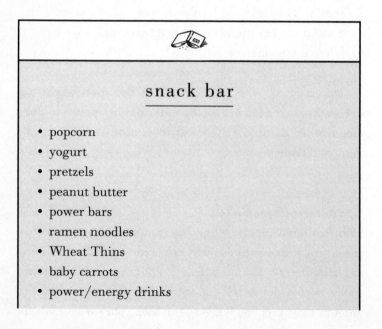

snack bar

- popcorn
- yogurt
- pretzels
- peanut butter
- power bars
- ramen noodles
- Wheat Thins
- baby carrots
- power/energy drinks

- milk
- coffee
- Gatorade
- Crystal Light
- Kool-Aid
- granola bars
- crackers
- canned or box soups
- bagels
- cream cheese
- dry cereal
- apples
- Pop-Tarts
- rice cakes
- nacho chips
- salsa
- Hi-C juice boxes
- macaroni-and-cheese packs

Refrigerators are the most popular room appliances. Rentals run $20–$45 per school year. Some students bring their own mini-refrigerators. Prices vary, but you can expect to pay around $100 for a new one. Other students said they purchased one in the spring from the senior hand-me-down sales circuit.

Redenbacher Wins

Microwave popcorn is the hands-down favorite snack. In the Midwest, Orville R's is judged the best—though most expensive—brand. "When we're really celebrating, we do an Orville."

Early Starts

Some students make it a point to get down for breakfast, as they feel it is the best meal of the day: The food is basic and identifiable.

> "Actually, breakfast is always very good. I get there early, even when I don't have an eight o'clock class."

Others study late, preferring to sleep in if they don't have an early class, and grab a Pop-Tart and Kool-Aid before hitting the road at 10 A.M. Baseball caps are clutch for bad hair days.

Container Clues

For Kool-Aid, you will need a quart jar with a lid on it. Buy the presweetened kind so all you have to do is add water and shake it up. For Crystal Light, you need a 2-quart container with a lid, as one little tub makes two quarts. Both of them are cheaper than soda pop. If you don't usually drink plain water, get in the habit. Buy a quart-size water bottle, fill it up, and chug it down by the end of the day.

Hot Pots, Etc.

Ramen noodles and Cup·A·Soup are popular snacks, because you just add water that you've heated in a hot pot or on a hot plate or with a heating coil. Toaster ovens are used to reheat last night's pizza, warm up bagels, and bake chocolate chip cookie dough that you buy in a tube. Some kids even bring bread machines, giving their dorm floors the aroma of a bakery.

weight

Freshman Fifteen

It's easy to put on the infamous freshman fifteen pounds, because snacking often seems to replace regular meals. Also, students tend to eat in order to avoid studying, to help them stay awake while studying, or to reward themselves for studying.

fats of life

Students who didn't gain weight attributed it to their regular eating habits and to avoiding or minimizing the intake of fats: butter or margarine, cheese, ice cream, mayonnaise, dips and chips, fries, doughnuts, and red meat. Eating lots of sweets is another way to put on extra pounds in a hurry.

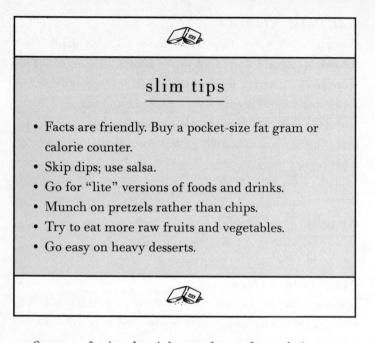

slim tips

- Facts are friendly. Buy a pocket-size fat gram or calorie counter.
- Skip dips; use salsa.
- Go for "lite" versions of foods and drinks.
- Munch on pretzels rather than chips.
- Try to eat more raw fruits and vegetables.
- Go easy on heavy desserts.

Some professional weight watchers rely on their mantra that nothing tastes as good as feeling thin feels, which could be true—with the possible exception of Ben & Jerry's New York Super Fudge Chunk ice cream.

anorexia and bulimia

While national health and nutrition experts continue to issue warnings that more than half of all Americans are overweight, one out of four college-age students struggles with some kind of eating disorder. Some young men may become anorexic or bulimic. However, young women are most prone to abusing their bodies by eating very little or by bingeing and then purging their bodies of food they have just consumed. Another common manifestation of someone with an eating disorder is obsessive running, exercising, or working out as a way to work off calories.

Counseling Help

Because eating disorders are so prevalent on college campuses today, many schools have counselors who are dedicated to educating and treating young men and women caught in the throes of these diseases. One counselor told us that the causes are complex, which means that recovery can entail a student getting help from a counselor, a nutritionist, *and* a physician.

> **"One of the causes is that young girls are bombarded with images of models, actresses, and rock stars who are grossly underweight. Constant media attention has turned these body images into the ideal. Some girls may find themselves scared about making the transition to womanhood. Others use not eating, or bingeing and purging, as a means of controlling the only thing they feel they can. Others may not eat so they can drink more. Just as stress can cause some people to overeat, it can have the opposite effect with someone afflicted with an eating disorder."**

Peer Support

One senior told us that her sorority no longer has private bathrooms, to discourage purging:

"There's a lot of pressure to look good, to make good grades, to try to fit in. It's stressful trying to hold everything together. For instance, someone may find out they are not going to make the kind of grades they did in high school, so it's a 'if I can't be the smartest one here, I can be the thinnest' kind of twisted thing."

While it is very hard for those who are dealing with these pressures and anxieties, a counselor pointed out that it is also very hard on their friends. Sometimes young women come to talk to her about a friend who has gone way beyond dieting into a full-time eating disorder, showing an almost paralyzing fear of gaining weight, and occasionally she will talk to a boyfriend who is very worried about his girlfriend's dramatic weight loss.

"I encourage them to ask them to come in or come with them so we can get them the help they need. In addition to talking with them to try to uncover the cause of their disorder, we try to get them to understand the enormous risk they are taking, that it can be fatal. We try to help them understand their body's basic nutritional needs. It's also important to get them involved in activities outside of academics that they really enjoy or care about—something they can get involved in with others to replace their constant focus on food. Having an eating disorder can be scary, shameful, and very isolating. They need to find a true friend, someone they can trust to help them on the road to recovery."

> ## TIP!
>
> To learn more about anorexia and bulimia and their treatment, here are two good websites: *http://www. edreferral.com/* and *http://www.something-fishy.org/ this.*

regular exercise

Almost everyone felt it was important to do some form of daily exercise. Former high school jocks, used to training two to three hours a day, said they were surprised at how they put on weight right away. The good news is that many schools have all kinds of intramural sports—tennis, basketball, indoor soccer, flag football, Ping-Pong, and ultimate Frisbee, among others.

> "They are fun and a great way to meet people. Lots of dorms and fraternities and sororities have their own teams. I had never played rugby before, but I decided to try it. Some teams get very competitive, but it is mostly just fun."

In addition to running, walking, biking, swimming, lifting weights, skating, or playing tennis, students mentioned two other popular forms of exercise:

- Aerobics: Many campuses hold free aerobics classes in their main athletic facility or in the basement of dorms. All you have to do is sign up or show up. Sometimes there is a minimal fee.

"I schedule myself in one at the end of my last class at four-thirty. It's a good way to get the kinks out and relieve stress."

- Super Circuit: This is available in many gyms. It's a forty-five-minute cardiovascular workout and gets good reviews for being quick, painless, and thorough.

"We have lighted basketball courts near our dorm. These are very popular spots, especially during finals. There is also a great athletic center with typical exercise equipment [leave your weights at home], along with pools, indoor basketball and tennis courts, and saunas."

Stress Busters

All of these forms of athletics or exercise are good (and legal) ways to deal with stress. Students cited dealing with roommates, feeling homesick, and becoming overwhelmed by the amount of class work as factors that can contribute to feeling stressed-out. Exercise can be a kind of mindless, nonverbal shutdown and chill-out time during your day, especially on weekends.

Breaking Away

While team sports seem to get the most attention in high school, college is a good time to begin making the shift to individual or "life" sports. For years now, a friend of mine has been returning to Iowa to bike the hot and crazy summer roads of RAGBRAI. When asked why he subjects himself to riding hundreds of miles over hill and dale under the summer sun, he replied, "Because when I'm riding my bike I don't have to be the best banker in the world."

sleep

Students say they sleep, on average, six to eight hours a night. *When* they sleep seems to vary and is not very predictable—it could occur from midnight to 6 or 7 A.M. or even from 3 A.M. to 9 or 10 A.M.

Power Naps

Whatever their nocturnal sleeping pattern, many students take power naps. These usually take place after lunch and can last anywhere from thirty minutes to two hours.

> "Usually these become even more powerful in the winter months."

Dead Times

The two hours in the late afternoon before the evening meal and the two hours afterward are often down or dead times.

This is when many extracurricular activities take place—sports, clubs, band and choral groups, theater groups, and so forth. Campus committee meetings are often scheduled late in the afternoon. Serious studying usually begins in the evening, sometime after dinner.

Escapes

When asked "What do you intend to do differently during your sophomore year?" one immediate response was:

> "Get some sleep. There are so many interesting distractions your freshman year. It's easy to take a study break around midnight and start talking to someone out in the hall. Then you decide to sit down outside in the hall and talk and suddenly it's three or four in the morning."

Some students go home for a weekend just to get caught up or get some "solid" sleep. One mother told me her daughter appeared at home, exhausted from midterms and pledge duties. "She must have slept fourteen hours straight. I found myself checking in on her just like when she was an infant, to make sure she was still breathing."

9.

money matters

Managing your finances, creating a budget, and living within your means are important skills to learn now, and they apply long after you graduate from college. In order to get a handle on your spending habits, you should begin to write down where your money goes. Get into the habit of keeping track of all of your expenses. Is this outrageously tedious? Of course. Will it be worth it in the long run? Definitely.

Second, before you go to college, sit down and talk to your parent/parents about spending guidelines. Use the monthly expense form (page 80) to help you anticipate the major categories of expenses. What part, if any, of these items will you be responsible for once you get to college? What can your parents afford to contribute to your day-to-day living expenses after making payments for your tuition, room and board, and student fees?

Together, you have to work out and agree to some initial

Monthly Expense Form

Cost of Tuition, Room and Board, and Fees

$ _____ Month _____ Year _____

---

1. School-Related Items—books, lab fees, high-powered calculator

2. Big-Ticket Items—loft, futon, bike, refrigerator

3. Food and Drink—ordering out, groceries

4. Personal—clothes, hair and body care

5. Entertainment—sporting events, movies, plays, CDs, videos/DVDs, magazines

6. Drug Store Items—toiletries, cosmetics

7. Long-Distance Phone Calls

8. Miscellaneous Expenses

guidelines that seem reasonable. After a couple of months on campus, you may have to reevaluate these, but at least you will begin with an agreed spending plan. Then look at what money will be available (yours and theirs). Between estimating what your expenses will be and how much money will be available to pay for them, you should be able to create a budget. Doing this financial planning is the easiest part of this process. Applying it is much harder. Learning to live within a budget takes discipline and effort and practice, but in the long run you'll be very glad you did.

When asked "What are you going to do differently your sophomore year?" one quick response was:

"Spend less money. Keep track of where it goes so I don't run out by Thanksgiving."

keeping track

How do students keep track of their expenses? In many different ways:

- One business major bought a ledgerlike notebook. She labels each page and records all expenditures for that group of items on the designated page.
- Another student bought a pack of 9 × 12 envelopes. He labels one envelope for each month. Then he records the amount of his purchase on the outside of the envelope and drops the sales slip inside. At the end of the month, he adds up the totals. This way, he can review all his monthly expenses at a glance. "An advantage to saving

receipts in one place is that if I need to return or
exchange an item, I can find the slip easily."
• Some students use software programs like
  Quicken to keep track of their expenditures.
  One of them started out doing that, but after a
  while, she got busy with classes and decided to
  just write down her day-to-day expenses in a small
  notebook.

Here's another method:

1. Drop all receipts for items purchased into some
    kind of container on your desk—a mug, stein, or
    small box.
2. At the end of each month, dump out all the slips.
3. Log in your expenses in the appropriate box on
    the monthly expense form (feel free to copy this).
4. Then add them up and record the totals in each
    box.
5. At the top of the expense form, you'll see one
    blank each for your tuition, room and board, and
    fees for the month. To get this monthly figure,
    divide your quarterly or semester bursar's bill by
    the appropriate number of months. (If you don't
    know the amount, ask your parents. They will
    be happy to share this raw data with you.) This
    gives you the fixed monthly cost of your basic
    college expenses.
6. Add this fixed cost to the totals in each of the
    boxes and you will have a good picture of
    the actual cost of attending college for that
    month.

You will note that the items in boxes 2–8 are discretionary expenses. This means you have ample opportunity to make choices and exercise judgment about how much you spend. Do I really need (fill in the blank) in order to achieve my personal goal of finding complete and total happiness and being at peace with the universe? Or is this something I just feel like buying?

Why Go to All the Trouble of Keeping Track of What You Spend?

If you are always running out of money, keeping track of expenditures allows you to review your monthly bills and see where you can cut back. You can begin to make choices about what things are important to you and what things can be eliminated. This could help you avoid spending money you don't have on things you don't need. It will also help you spot—and avoid—spending pitfalls:

buying items on impulse

buying things on sale because they seem too good a deal to pass up

buying duplicate items you don't need but you just like to buy—software, lipstick, another pair of sweats, etc.

skipping the cafeteria, where your meal is already paid for, and ordering pizza instead

SURPRISE!
Several students were surprised at the cost of textbooks. The typical cost for first-semester classes ran $400–$500.

"My math book wasn't immediately available. So we had to use the online text. This was confusing when it would say, 'Refer back to page ten.' I was glad when we got the print version two weeks into the course, but was sad that it cost ninety-five dollars."

TIP!

One student suggests buying used books instead of new ones. "I now buy a new one only if it is related to my major or it's one that I know I will want to keep. Otherwise, I buy used books and resell them when I've finished the course."

---

banking

As with choosing a service for making long-distance phone calls, there are lots of banking options, with many variables. You need to find the one that best fits your situation and needs. This may mean starting out with one method and then discovering a better system.

Some students open a checking account at home. Others find it easier to wait and open one at a bank or college credit union once they are on campus. Some have both—an account at home in case a parent needs to make an emergency deposit and one on campus for their day-to-day expenses. Many financial institutions offer special student accounts, featuring low fees for maintaining a minimum balance, convenient ATMs used mainly for withdrawing cash, and overdraft protection if the checking account is combined with a savings account.

Nearly all checking accounts provide you with a check-cashing card. By keying in your PIN (personal identification number) you can access cash via ATM machines.

TIP!

Don't keep your PIN number with your card in your billfold. Memorize it or log it into your personal data file. You want to be the only person able to withdraw money from your account. Keep the paper receipt the machine will kick out along with the cash. Deduct your withdrawal from your checking account balance. (If you use an ATM to make a deposit into your account, you also need to save the receipt.)

Plan ahead for your cash needs. Don't access an ATM at night, especially if you are by yourself.

Debit Cards

You may also be able to use your bank card as a debit card. Using it this way means that when you make a purchase, the amount is automatically deducted from your checking account. This saves you the trouble of writing a check. Again, be sure to keep the receipt so that you can write down the deduction in your checking account register. That way, you'll know the money isn't there anymore.

Paper Trail

If you are using a checking account for the first time, it may be easier to write a paper check and immediately record it in the check register. Or you can order checks that have a carbon, so you will have a copy of the ones you have written. If your checkbook becomes all messed up and you are not sure what your actual balance is, ask your bank or credit union to run a printout of all your recent transactions. This service may cost a few bucks, but it is a *lot* cheaper than paying the fine for a bounced check.

Online Banking

If you are comfortable with doing banking online, many financial institutions provide this service free. You will be issued a PIN number for accessing your account. This will allow you to pull up your account online, view checks that have been cleared or deposits made, and transfer money from your savings account to your checking account. The trick here is to remember your PIN number. The other trick is to avoid having the system down when you want to perform a transaction.

Monthly Statement

You will receive a monthly statement from your financial institution that lists all your transactions for the month. It is your record of the checks you have written that have cleared (i.e., been cashed), what cash withdrawals you might have made at an ATM, and what purchases you have paid for with your debit card. If you have made any deposits during that thirty-day period, they will show up, too. Be sure to keep all your teller or ATM receipts until you receive your monthly statement. This is the only existing proof that you have made a deposit. Also, when you make a deposit, be sure to use the slips that come with your checks: They have your account number printed on them.

Balancing Your Account

On the back of the statement, you will usually find directions on how to balance or reconcile your account. This means finding out how much money you *really* have in your account. This is not difficult if you have recorded the amounts of checks you have written past the date of the statement (called "outstanding" checks) and if you have saved the receipts from ATM or debit-card transactions. Simply add up all these and subtract them from the balance shown on your statement. If you have made any deposits to your account after the date of the statement, add these to that number. The result is your real balance. It's a good idea to reconcile your account each month after you receive your statement.

> ## TIP!
>
> "I'd advise a freshman not to carry around a lot of
> cash, for obvious reasons. Write checks, use a debit
> card, and carry a small amount of cash for daily ex-
> penses. Also, I started with having my checking ac-
> count at home, but I later switched to opening an
> account on campus. Although I could use an ATM
> with my home account, there was a service charge of
> two dollars each time I did. Now that I have my ac-
> count here on campus, I don't have to pay to make a
> withdrawal."

Many large banks have branches and ATM machines in
a number of states. This is another way to avoid having to
pay a fee to access money via an ATM machine.

credit cards

Don't be surprised if you begin to get bunches of credit-card
offers in the mail, even before you leave for college. On campus, be prepared to be besieged.

> "Credit card hawkers come up to you everywhere,
> even when you are studying. They'll give you a free
> T-shirt if you fill out an application."

Warning—It's too easy to get hooked and slide down the
slippery slope of "buy now and pay later." Let's say you find

a really cool mountain bike on sale for only $400. You bring out the plastic and it's yours in a matter of seconds. Your charge card has an annual interest rate of 18%. You make the minimum 2% payment each month. At this rate, it will take you only 62 months (over 5 years) to own the bike outright. If you would like to know what the bike would actually end up costing you (18% over 5 years), check out *http://www.bankrate.com/brm/calc/MinPayment.asp?nav= cc&page=calc.*

Suggested Options

Trash all credit-card offers until you get a real job.

Get only one card for emergencies. Do your homework and find a card with no annual fee.

Get only one card and use it sparingly. Pay off the full balance at the end of each month. It is possible to "freeze" your credit-card limit so that your card is good for charges only up to that limit. For example, if you freeze your card at $500, you will not be able to charge items over that amount.

Establishing Credit

If you do use a credit card and pay off your balance on a regular and timely basis, this is a good way to establish credit. However, if you don't, be aware that a bad record stays on your credit report for seven years. This will make it hard for you to obtain any kind of loan. It will also make it very difficult to get the best interest rates available.

Many students get one or more cards and don't pay off their balances. They end up in deep credit-card debt. Because of this, some colleges no longer allow card vendors on campus.

part-time work

Give yourself time to adjust to your new college environment. Unless it is a financial necessity, avoid taking on a part-time job until after your first year. You will find that being out of money is a common college experience.

> "I go to the psychology labs whenever I'm low on cash. They are always tracking rapid eye movements or something. Other kids cut hair, type papers, give pedicures, or do laundry for extra money. One real entrepreneur makes chili and sells it on Sunday nights."

financial aid

Many students receive some form of financial aid. It may be based on need or merit or both. Here's some inside advice from a financial aid officer at a private college:

> **"We send out two forms to students in January— the government form and our own. The students receive these four to six months in advance so that they have plenty of time to gather the information required to meet the application deadline. Still, it's amazing how lax some students are about get-**

ting their applications in on time. My key advice: Deadlines matter! Returning your forms on time can mean the difference between getting money or not. If a student misses a deadline, all the scholarship money could be gone."

FAFSA

The government form is called the FAFSA (Free Application for Federal Student Aid). Because this is a very detailed form, many states have representatives from colleges visit high schools to explain what kinds of funds are available and how to fill out the form properly. These information sessions are held in the evening or sometimes on weekends, so that parents can attend. It's a good idea if you all go together so that you will learn the purpose and details of the required information.

Both you and your parents must complete this form to apply for federal student aid. Some colleges will require you to fill out their own form as well. Your high school guidance department is a good source of information on all the scholarships, loans, and grants.

TIP!

The FAFSA form will require your parents' and your (if you need to file) tax information. It is important for you and your parent/parents to file early in the year so that you'll have all the information needed to fill out the FAFSA for your college's financial aid office. Remember, those who hesitate—or procrastinate—could lose out on college dollars.

Good Relationship Advice

One financial aid officer we interviewed said it was important for students to establish a good relationship with their adviser.

> **"Make that person your ally. If a financial crisis occurs at home—a parent loses his or her job or is laid off—go see your adviser right away. Explain that your financial support situation has changed. Don't wait until your bills are due or past due. If you anticipate a problem, see someone sooner rather than later. The more time we have to work with the student to put together a new plan, the better."**

Work-Study

Some of the students we interviewed qualified for work-study. This is a need-based form of federal financial aid, based on family income. If you qualify for work-study, be sure to consider using it as a part of your financial aid package.

> "The great thing about this program is that everyone wants to hire these students. Because the government subsidizes the students' salaries, departments that may not have money to hire students are then able to, given the help from the government. This means that all departments are interested in federal work-study students, so they are often in high demand and have more job choice than those without it."

Other Scholarship Deadlines

Thousands of private and corporate foundations, civic organizations, and individual trust funds award scholarships each year. If you have received a scholarship from one of these groups that is renewable, based on maintaining a certain GPA, send in a copy of your transcript as soon as you receive your grades. One foundation director told us:

> "We expect our scholarship winners to initiate this renewal process. We tell them we won't be sending them a 'please send us your grades' reminder each spring. It is their responsibility to get the information to us if they want to receive their scholarship money for the following year."

Student Loans

Many students must apply for student loans in addition to scholarships and government aid. If you may need to do this, here are some excellent tips from a recent college graduate to help you:

"I would urge students to shop around for student loans. Not all student loans are the same. Some lenders offer reduced fees, different interest rates, or other incentives. So it is worth it to do some comparison lender shopping and not just go with a local financial institution. You might find better loans if you take the time to look around.

"Be aware of lender fees, interest rates, and terms of repayment when considering a loan. Some federal loans have subsidized interest while you're in school. That's the kind of loan you should borrow from first. With other loans, you could start incurring interest while you're in school. When you start repayment after you've graduated from college, you're starting off with a lot more debt than you thought.

"This is down the road, but when your loans go into repayment, there's usually no prepayment penalty. [Be sure to check on this before you take out the loan.] This means you can pay off the principal of the loan quicker, without being responsible for all the interest the loan should have incurred from the time you first borrowed it. If you get any kind of bonus when you start your first job, or during it, consider paying off some of the principal. It really does make a difference in the overall amount you will end up having to repay.

"My final piece of advice would be to try to keep all of your loans with the same lender. This makes repayment much easier. You have just one check to write each month instead of having to write several checks to several lenders. Also, by borrowing money from just one source, there is a very good chance your repayments will be lower."

TRUE STORY

"My junior year I borrowed a relatively small amount—$1,000—from a different lender than the one I used during my first two years. I did this because I thought the loan might be processed more quickly. In my senior year, I borrowed again from the lender I used my first two years.

"When my loans went into repayment after I graduated, I ended up paying $50 a month on the $1,000 loan. But I was paying a lot less than $50 a month (per $1,000) with my other lender. I found out later that the minimum repayment was $50 a month, so that's why I had to pay so much on the $1,000 loan. For my other loan, which totaled $17,000, I was paying only $230 a month. It may not seem like much, but when you are starting your first job, you really want to save where you can."

Credit Rating

Just as repaying a balance on a credit card on a regular basis each month will help you establish a good credit rating, so will paying off your student loans. Keep in mind that you may not need to borrow everything that is offered in your financial aid package.

If you find you can work more hours in college and earn more money, you don't have to borrow all the money that is available to you right away. In other words, don't borrow just because it is offered. Be sure you need the money.

After you graduate and begin paying off your loans, doing so on time will help you establish good credit if you also want to borrow money to buy a car, make a down payment on a house or condo, and so forth. Also, it could reduce the interest rate on the loan. After forty-eight months of your making scheduled payments on time, a lender may reduce the interest rate so that your loan can be paid off sooner than you had originally planned. This is a good thing.

Financial Aid Sites

If you are interested in learning more about financial aid for college, here are two good sites:

www.finaid.org: The site opens with a well-designed summary of the variety of sources of financial aid. Click on the links to read the details.

www.ed.gov: This is the Department of Education's site. It provides a wealth of information about government aid programs. The Student Guide to Financial Aid is updated each year.

10.

long-distance

E-mail, voice mail, beepers, and faxes are changing the way we communicate, but they are all one-way streets. Picking up the phone to hear the sound of someone's voice remains an old but popular way to stay in touch.

"Sometimes you just need to talk to someone."

choices

Fortunately, there are a number of popular options to choose from. Before you select your long-distance system, ask yourself these questions: Who are the people I will want to call? Do they live in state or out of state? How often will I want to call them? When will I most likely want to give them a call? The answers to these questions will give you some data points that will help you make a decision.

Traditional Long-Distance Service

Different colleges are on different systems. Some provide a phone in each room for local and long-distance use. One student who recently moved into his dorm at a large university reported:

> "There is a phone jack in each room, but you have to bring your own phone. You'll also want to bring and hook up an answering machine. For long-distance calls, my roommate and I each got a PIN number, so long-distance calls are automatically billed to the right person. No hassling over the bill. It worked well. We got our phone number the same day we moved in. I haven't used it to call long-distance yet, but I've heard the rates are pretty reasonable."

General Guidelines

Whether you call via the service provided in your room or you choose a different option, there are two rules that generally apply. The most expensive times to call are during the day and during the week. This is when America does business. Whether using a land line or a wireless phone, the cheapest times to call are usually nights and weekends. Find out what your company's rate structure is—i.e., when do nights and weekends start and end?

Example: If you use a cell phone that offers free long-distance on nights after 9:00 P.M., don't call at 8:59 or you will be charged the day rate. Also, be careful not to answer your cell phone before 9:00.

"I always tell people to call me on my cell at nine-ten,
just to be sure."

AVOID!

The second important thing to know is that the most expensive calls are the operator-assisted ones: information, collect,
person-to-person, and third-party calls. These can be ridicu-
lously expensive.

One parent told us she had two sons at two different
schools and ended up getting an 800 number instead of having them call collect. "They both have access to a set of PIN
numbers so they can reach me or their father at home or at
work. They can also use it to call each other. I didn't want
them to think they couldn't afford to call home or each
other."

Prepaid Calling Cards

If you are on a budget and want to keep your calls under a
certain amount per month, buying a phone card is a good
choice. These are available for a varying number of minutes
and you can buy them almost everywhere. It pays to shop for
the card with the best rate—the lowest cost per minute.
Every time you punch in your PIN number, you'll find out
how many minutes you have left. Then you can either
renew that card or buy another one. Several students said
they received phone cards in their graduation cards and
thought they made a great gift.

Cell Phones

Five years ago, cell phones on campus were rare. Now most students depend on them for making their long-distance calls. Many wireless companies offer special monthly rates within a certain radius, free night and weekend calls, a rollover feature for any unused minutes, and family-plan options with reduced rates for additional phones or lines. It can be an amazing maze of rates and options.

TIP!

To compare wireless companies' features, rates, and roaming charges—or just to learn the terminology—check out MyRatePlan.com. It contains comprehensive information and it's free. Because special rates and deals change quickly, beware of long-term contracts. You also want to avoid getting locked into a bunch of services you really won't need.

TRUE STORY

If you do carry a cell phone, be sure to turn it off when you are in class.

"I have a brother who is twelve years older than me. He wanted to know how I was holding up during my first week of classes. He called me right in the middle of my first day in a large lecture class, Psych 101. I was so embarrassed. My phone was in the bottom of my backpack, and I had to fumble around before I found it and turned it off. I never took it with me to class again."

Standard Time

It's a good idea to set a standard calling time with people you'll call regularly. Some students called home at a designated time.

"I check in with my parents on weekends, usually early Sunday afternoon. That way we don't miss each other all the time or end up exchanging answering-machine messages."

Long-Distance Relationships

Students with the highest phone bills were those who were going with someone back home or at another school. Their advice: *Avoid phone fights!*

"I always need to get things settled. One of my calls to my boyfriend ended up lasting two and a half hours, prime time. The bill was horrendous!"

TRUE NEW STORY

A newspaper ran a story about a freshman who "borrowed" his dad's business phone and took it with him to college. He was very homesick for his girlfriend and called her every night. Evidently, he didn't call home much, to avoid raising suspicion. So his dad was surprised when his employer promptly handed over the bill to him for the last quarter of the year: It was for $11,783.

TRUE OLD STORY

One first-year student called her HTH (hometown honey) every night. By Christmas her phone bill was $700. Her parents told her she would have to sell her car to pay off her bill. It is now twenty years and four children later, so all those calls did eventually lead somewhere. I saw her recently at the grocery store and asked if I could use her story. "Oh yes, but don't tell my kids." And then she added wistfully, "It was a great car."

Do students ever write letters or send postcards anymore?

> "I'm sure a few people still do, but mostly they stay connected through e-mail or instant messaging. I mail out cards for birthdays or whenever I find one that reminds me of someone. Everyone likes to get mail."

> "Writing a letter these days seems very personal, private. You can write one wherever you are. And it's wonderful to find one in your mailbox."

11.

computers @ campus

It's almost impossible to exaggerate the impact computers have had on education. The PC was introduced in 1984, so most of you have grown up with computers and the Internet. You already use e-mail and instant messaging, do Web searches, and perhaps download music files from the Net. When you get to college, you'll find computers everywhere. You'll also find that information technology plays a role in almost every aspect of academic life. One professor reported,

> "Since students use the Internet for so much of their research, I'm afraid our libraries are becoming underused. It is much easier for them to seek out sources on Google than hunt down references elsewhere.
>
> "It also affects how information is passed outside the classroom. Before e-mail, I would get calls

from students at three A.M., when they knew I wouldn't be in my office. They would use voice mail to notify me that they wouldn't be in class or that they were sick or that a paper would be late. Now they use e-mail. It makes everyone instantly accessible. It's easier for me to get in touch with them, too, if I have to give them new information about a class or assignment. I have a class distribution list, so I can notify them all at once of a change in schedule or remind them of an outside lecture or speaker coming in."

Computer Basics

All campuses will have computers and printers for your personal use. You may find a small computer lab in your dorm and larger labs located in buildings all around campus. Although some colleges require freshmen to bring their own computers, the majority do not. However, many students find it is more convenient to have their own. Here's some information that may be helpful before you make a decision.

There are three types of computers on campus: PCs (personal computers, formerly known as IBM compatibles, most of which are Windows-based machines), Macintoshes (computers made by Apple Computer—iMacs, iBooks, etc.), and workstations. You really only need to concern yourself with the first two. If you are thinking about bringing your own computer to school, you need to find out which type of computer your school supports—Apple or IBM. Most software programs are cross-platformed (that is, they work on both types, provided you have the proper software installed), but it doesn't hurt to check out which platform your school prefers.

TIP!

If you are thinking of buying a computer to take to college, be aware that some schools have contracts with computer companies, so you may be able to purchase one at a special discount. If not, shop around. There's a familiar saying that your computer is out of date as soon as you buy it. But find one that fits your basic needs. Don't think that all the new bells and whistles are academic necessities.

If you are bringing your own computer and printer or sharing one with a roommate, be sure to pack a five-outlet surge protector. Use your ingenuity to keep the wires together so you won't trip over them in your room. Different types of cable organizers are available (one student reports that duct tape works just fine). Check before you buy an Ethernet cord to plug into the school's network. Usually, the right type is provided as part of their package.

Introductory Classes

Since students come to college with varying degrees of familiarity with computers, most schools offer short introductory classes on the basic skills you will need. They also include an explanation of the school's network.

"I'd highly advise freshmen to take an intro course if one is offered."

In addition to courses, many schools have computer consultants in the large labs. They are there to help you with problems you may have. We interviewed a consultant who gave this advice:

"Don't be afraid to ask for help. Your question may seem dumb to you, but be assured: It's been asked before. We are being paid to answer questions, and none are too simple. I actually like the easy ones. It builds my self-esteem, so that I can tackle the really challenging ones that are sure to follow."

Your R.A. will most likely be a good source for learning basic computer operations, like how to open your e-mail account, how to connect to the school's network, how to send something from your computer to a printer located in a lab, and how to save files on a server for easy access. Some residence halls may even have a live-in computer guru to help you. If someone on your floor is a tech-head and has lots of hands-on computer experience or is majoring in computer science, make a point of becoming friends.

Uses of Computers

You may be able to sign up for your classes on the Net, view your schedule and bursar's bill, and look up all kinds of campus directories, intramural activities, bus schedules, library hours, etc. Some of your professors may have their lectures available as PowerPoint presentations and may ask you to print a copy ahead of time to better utilize class time. Many post assignments, suggest links and articles, and ask for you to submit your assignments via the computer. One student told us:

> "We get our non—essay type test results on the Net, usually just hours after we've finished taking them. That kind of immediacy can be a mixed blessing."

By far the biggest use of computers is in doing research and writing papers.

> "I'd say doing research on the computer is essential. It's convenient and it's free. Some of the links are extremely long, so it does take time to go through them."

But there are downsides to using the Web. One professor said,

> "For one thing, not everything on the Net is true. There is the whole 'legitimacy of information' question. Secondly, I encourage my students to check out many sources when they are working on a project or paper. Some of them think that if they can't do the research on the Web, it's not worth doing. They miss other valuable print sources."

Plagiarism

Because there are so many research papers and book reports on the Web, plagiarism continues to receive attention. Most students realize that downloading a file and copying anything verbatim without crediting the source is wrong. It is just as unethical to not credit an electronic source as it is a written one. If you steal an idea or interpretation from a paper or an article and simply put it in your own words or rearrange paragraphs, it is still plagiarism.

TRUE STORY

"I taught English to college-bound seniors long before the Internet. My first semester of teaching, I flunked about half my students in one class on a major theme. They had used CliffsNotes or another very popular interpretation of *Macbeth.* It caused an uproar. Students claimed a) they didn't know it was wrong to use just a few sentences, or b) they were so bogged down with other classwork and outside activities they didn't have time to do their own work. The principal received calls from complaining parents. My response was that it was better for kids to learn the consequences of cheating in high school rather than discover it in college. In my final semester of college, two students in my senior-lit seminar were caught plagiarizing in their final papers. They didn't graduate.

"I hope you have received better information on citing sources in your high school, where

honor codes exist and formal plagiarism policies
are enforced. Be aware that teachers now have
sites like *TurnItIn.com* and *Plagiarism.com*. These
programs can track papers for similar vocabulary,
sentence structure, and ideas to detect and deter
plagiarism. They also help protect intellectual
property and copyrights. So although there are
countless term papers on popular websites, there
are also increasingly sophisticated online data-
bases to track them down."

TIP!

Do your own research and write your own papers.
Also, save, and save often.

One senior we interviewed said,

"Everyone has lost work because the computer
crashed or they didn't save properly. My first three
years at school I lost a lot of work. By my senior year
I finally wised up. I saved everything connected with
my senior thesis on my hard drive and on disk. Fortunately, I never lost any of my papers. Also, it's important to put your disk in a protective case. Don't just
get in a hurry and throw your disk into your backpack if you plan to work on it at another computer
location on campus. It's your work and effort—
protect it."

12.

studying

"What one thing do you wish someone would have told you about before going to college?" Student responses to this question varied. Nearly half of them talked about the new academic level they encountered their first semester and the effort required to reach this new level.

a whole new level

Three of those interviewed had been high school valedictorians, no slackers indeed. So it was surprising to learn that even these straight-A students felt unprepared for the kind of work college-level courses required. Two of them went to private schools, one to a state university.

"It doesn't matter where you go. College anywhere is going to be a couple of notches above high school work. Everyone needs help to make the big transition."

———

"You'll know after your first test how you are doing or not doing. I found that my high school days of quick cramming or cruising through material the night before a test were gone for good."

———

"I was really surprised when I got my first C. I made mostly A's in high school. It was in a chemistry course, which was required for my major. Then I learned my prof had had his wife in class and flunked her twice, so I didn't feel too bad."

———

"I was totally clueless about how much time I would have to spend studying. My first test was a real wake-up call. I got only 60 out of 100 points. Everyone struggles with the amount of studying it takes."

———

"I expected the bigger workload. What was stressful to me was the lack of feedback. There were not many grades to help me know if I was doing well or interpreting the information correctly. This was pretty stressful the first semester."

———

"One of the hardest things for me my first year was realizing that studying for college and studying in high school are worlds apart. There is so much to adjust to—new city, new friends, new responsibilities—that your GPA is usually the first to suffer. Many counselors said that it's typical for your GPA to either go up a point or drop down a point from high school during the first semester at college. Rarely does it stay the same. But it's early in your career, so you have plenty of time to bring it back up."

—

"I studied hard in high school so I could be admitted here, or at least I thought I did. I would study five hours for big exams my senior year in high school. I learned it took four or five times that amount of effort in college."

—

"To me the big difference is that in high school you could do well reading the material and memorizing facts. In college you're expected to:

- Think critically on your own.
- Ask questions.
- Explore implications.
- Make connections.

"It's the whole 'ideas, issues, values' thing."

—

"In my first paper in English lit, the assignment was to write about why, at the end of *The Canterbury Tales*, Chaucer recanted everything he had written. I thought I turned in a really good paper, for sure, an A. When I got it back, I got a B−. The prof wrote that it was well written but that I hadn't expressed any ideas that he hadn't presented in class. He wanted to know what *I* thought. After that, I tried to come up with my own interpretation and go with it, even if it seemed far-out. They'd rather hear an interesting idea than a well-written summary of their own."

"There's just so much reading!"

"I liked the challenge. I'm a hard worker."

"You always hear there are these easy courses out there to help raise your grade point average—Rocks for Jocks and Physics for Poets. Don't waste your time looking. There are no easy courses."

where to study

Students seem to divide themselves into two groups: those who study mainly in their rooms and those who study somewhere else. A disadvantage to room work is that there are many distractions—phones ringing, loud music, people dropping in.

"If I stay in my room, I sometimes end up just gazing at my posters or photos from home, looking at my closet and wondering what I'm going to wear tomorrow, finding myself drawn to other books on my shelf that I'd rather be reading than my current assignment, or being drawn to that great magnet—the *bed!*"

Room Dwellers

Successful room dwellers said they prefer studying in their room because they can totally relax, and they like having all their papers, notes, and books in one place. Some who studied here said they literally locked themselves in their room, took the phone off the hook, and left a note on their door saying when they would be taking a break. Others reported turning their answering machines on and getting good at telling kids who stopped by that they were seriously study-ing and would catch up with them later.

> "You don't have to lug a bunch of stuff to the library, or get there and find you've left something you need back at the dorm."

Studying Out

Those who chose to study out said it was mainly so they could concentrate without so many interruptions. However, one student pointed out that not all libraries are the answer:

> "Some libraries can become more socializing centers than places to do serious work. People just go there to hang out, meet people, or be seen. It doesn't take long to figure out which ones those are."

Other libraries can be silent safe havens. Usually, centers that are open twenty-four hours a day are more conducive to serious studying.

> "The only way I can really get focused is to head off to a library and away from all distractions."

> "During finals week I was spending so much time at the library I ended up taking my toothbrush."

Both

Some dorms have a large study area in the basement. Others may turn their cafeteria area into study tables at night. If these kinds of facilities are available, you can leave your room, go downstairs, and then take a break.

> "I study down in our cafeteria. Then when I want to take a break, I go back up to my room and check my e-mail or phone messages."

Study Table

Most sororities and fraternities have evening study tables for pledges. Students who pledged said that although study table was mandatory and they naturally resisted it at first, it ended up being very helpful.

> "I studied much more in the [frat] house than I would have if I'd been on my own."

Total Absorption

Two students said they found a library with small enclosures or carrels where they would hole up before big tests.

> "It became a helpful psychological device for me. Whenever I was in that place, the only thing I would do was study. I had no other mental association with it. I would take a short break, go walk around outside, or listen to my Walkman for a while. Then I would be refreshed and ready to go back and hit the books."

study breaks

Everyone maintains that you have to be realistic on the front end. Plan to take short breaks: "Don't think you can study four to six hours straight through," said one student.

Watch out for extended breaks, though.

> "Some kids stop studying on Thursday night and won't crack a book until Sunday night. There is no way anyone taking a full load of classes can keep up with everything on that kind of routine."

additional help

There are different kinds of study groups formed on some campuses, especially for tough techy courses in calculus, physics, and chemistry. One engineering student told us: "I took one of the help courses in chemistry my freshman year. It was for one hour of credit and met three evenings a week. The leaders really knew the material and the profs. It helped me a lot, especially before exams." A student at a smaller school echoed those thoughts:

> "There is all kinds of help available. No one should see these classes as remedial or dumb. They are for any student smart enough to know they need help."

Study Groups or Partners

Large classes may have study groups you can participate in to help review material before exams. Sometimes finding a study partner is useful.

"I didn't do well on my first calculus exam. So I went to see my professor. She was very helpful and worked through all the problems with me. She suggested I team up with another girl in the class. We worked the problems separately, then met for two or three hours the night before class to compare answers and explain to each other how we arrived at them. It was a great help."

One student struggling with math made an interesting point about how math differs from other subjects. "If you are reading a novel, you might not understand why a character does or says something. You can just put a question mark in the margin and read on. Or if you are studying a foreign language and come across a word or phrase you don't know the meaning of, you circle it and keep reading. If you get stuck in math, you just have to stop. There is no way to just skip over a step and keep going."

TIP!

If you get stuck, get help.

Learning Centers

There are also non-credit kinds of help courses available at some schools via their computer network. Another possible source of help could be a teaching or learning center.

> "Our center has really good short courses in speed-reading, learning how to ask questions, and learning how to develop better study habits."

A student on one campus said he didn't discover the Center for Teaching and Learning until the last semester of his senior year.

> "This was unfortunate. I could have used the techniques I learned all through school. I took a course when I discovered I was one credit hour short of having enough to graduate.
> "My best advice to new students is: Don't play it down to the wire. Build in some buffer so you will be sure to have more than enough credits to graduate."

> "One of the techniques I learned was called question-driven concept busting. I use it all the time now at work. It relies on a self-coaching method. You identify a problem and ask questions, try a new approach, figure out what changed, what worked, what didn't."

Initiative

One student emphasized the importance of getting help early: "I'd advise a freshman to ask a counselor, academic adviser, or the professor about any course that is causing a problem. It's important to take the initiative and not wait until it's too late. There is usually outside help available, but you need to be aggressive and seek assistance on your own."

comp 101

Since being able to communicate your ideas verbally and in writing is so important, most schools require freshmen to take Composition 101. The purpose is to help students both with the mechanics and the content of their writing. Writing can be a real stumbling block for many who have grown up with e-mail and instant messaging. If most of your written communication has been quick, filled with codes, abbreviations, and techno-shorthand, you'll need to learn to slow down. Also, don't forget to use the spell-check feature of your word-processing program.

TRUE STORY

> **"A student sent me a three-line e-mail asking if he could get into my class. It contained three spelling errors. I replied that he could still get into the class, but I hoped this was not an example of the quality of his writing."**

We interviewed a professor who teaches writing to freshmen to seek some good tips. She explained:

> **"Students often hand in papers that are technically correct (spelling, grammar, punctuation, complete sentences, etc.), but they don't under-**

stand when I give them a C. So I've learned this is the best way to explain how I evaluate the contents of a paper.

"C: Thinking literally—This shows they have read the text and have a basic understanding. They know what major points or key ideas the author is trying to convey.

"B: Thinking inferentially—They are able to connect ideas to other ones. They are able to derive or infer something from the original information given.

"A: Thinking analytically—They understand the text, break things down, connect ideas, examine the implications, and draw conclusions."

Writing Tutorials

The professor also stressed that many campuses offer writing tutorials to help students:

"We tracked students who visited the writing center just once a week. The majority improved their grade by one full letter. I'm also encouraged when a student cares enough to come and see me for help during my office hours. At first some seem almost apologetic. I always tell them I've been waiting all semester for you to stop by. That's why I'm here."

writing papers

One of the hardest things to learn is gauging the effort and how much time it will take to write a paper. It is always better to allow yourself more time than you think you will need.

First Drafts

"I learned to try to find out what style of paper a prof was looking for, especially the first one in a class. I would ask if she had a sample of an A paper I could review—not on my own topic, of course—so that I could get a sense of her expectations."

Another thing to be aware of is that in some classes you may be able to submit a first draft and receive feedback to improve your final version. One student said, "Now, whenever I'm not sure if I'm on the right track or not, I ask if the professor will take a look at my first draft."

Peer Help

"I've always felt unsure of my writing, so I ask peers to read over my papers and get their reactions. Does it make sense? Do they get my point? Are my spelling and grammar correct? An English major down the hall helped me a lot."

> **TIP!**
>
> Try reading your paper out loud to hear how it flows.
> This is a good way to catch run-on sentences.

study tips and techniques

Here are some good suggestions from the many students we
interviewed:

- "I read the material straight through. Then I go
  back and highlight. Then I take notes on what
  I've highlighted. I create my own study guide."
- "I find that I retain material better if I highlight
  as I read and then go back and review what I've
  highlighted."
- An engineering student who is dyslexic reports, "I
  try to spend an hour or two reading what the prof
  is going to cover before I go to the lecture. That
  way I read it, then hear it, and then write down
  the key points by taking notes. After class, I
  review my notes to see if I've understood what
  I've written. Eventually it begins to sink in."
- "I read the text and highlight as I go along. Then
  I take notes on what I've read. Then I go to class
  and take lecture notes. Then I type up both sets of
  notes and use them to review."
- "Our prof has his lectures on PowerPoint, so we
  don't have to take notes. He said he wants our full

attention when we are in class. We can print the notes out later."

- "It's important to understand that class starts on the first day and to begin to take good notes right away. There's no drifting into the subject. Why did it take me so long to figure that out?"

- Two students said the most important thing to learn your first year is to stop by and visit your T.A. or prof. "It's important to let them know who you are and that you are interested in the course."

- Another student said he saw that classmates who spent time getting to know the T.A.s consistently received a half- or full grade higher. "Now I know. They have office hours. Take advantage of them. They don't tell you what is on the test, although they know that. But they can tell you what areas to focus on, and they answer questions you might have on the lecture."

Clues

Everyone processes and absorbs new information in different ways and at different speeds. You may need to experiment to discover which study techniques are right for you.

Is it important to you to see the instructor, observe facial expressions, gestures, and body language? If so, be brave. Sit up front.

Does taking notes during lectures help you to concentrate? Or do ideas sink in better when you just listen? Can you make up a class by getting someone else's notes, or do you count on remembering some things just by hearing?

Deadweek

Many schools have a week before final exams when there are no classes. This is officially known as deadweek. It may be formally ushered in, with all students screaming at the top of their lungs in unison everywhere on campus at midnight.

Final Exams

Here are some suggestions on preparing for finals: Keep all your notes, homework, tests, and quizzes together. One student suggests buying a pack of clear plastic sheet protectors. These come already punched so that they fit into a three-ring binder. They are open on the top, allowing you to store tests inside and keep them together with your class notes.

Start your review process for finals early.

"I don't cram well or do well under pressure. So I create my own study schedule, figure how much I will have to cover in each class, and block off that time on my study calendar two or three weeks in advance."

"In some classes you will cover so much material that it is easy to forget what you covered at the beginning of the quarter. So allow yourself more time to review the early material. Star in your notes what the prof seemed most excited about. Usually, they'll ask something about it on the final."

Most profs will give you a pre-final review and tell you what is important. If not, don't be afraid to ask: "What specific areas will be covered? Where should my focus be?"

Anxiety Control

"I always sat in the same seat toward the front in big lecture classes. When I went in for the final exam, I sat there. It felt normal. Also, I got dressed up for the final, just as if I were going to a normal class. It was good for me psychologically. A lot of kids just grunge out and wear the same thing all week."

Many students said it was important to eat right during finals week and avoid all-nighters, which can wipe you out for the next couple of days. If you try to keep a reasonable schedule, there is a remote possibility that during finals week you can lead a normal life.

"I treat myself by going to see a movie after taking a final before I start studying for the next one. It's important to cut yourself some slack."

"Don't go over each problem or question with someone after the final is over. You'll end up getting upset about a little step you screwed up on, which made your whole problem, program, or point you were trying to make turn out wrong. It's better to forget it and go on with something else. Besides, you never know what the curve is going to look like. You may have done okay after all. Just move on."

Be Advised

You will always run into kids who are extremely bright. They don't go to class or study much. They can whip out papers in the time it takes to type them. If they are rich and have flawless complexions, avoid them on bad days. College, like life, is not fair. Good advice for the vast majority:

- Show up for class.
- Pay attention.
- Take notes.
- Ask questions.
- Study for tests.
- Let go of the results.

Good News

Developing your own good study habits your freshman year pays off.

"Once I got into my major, everything began falling into place. I was in a good groove. Studying was much easier. I'm doing well now."

13.

social life

Adapting to a new academic environment and learning to manage your time are a big part of settling in during your first year. However, the major challenge by far is adjusting to a totally new social scene.

first impressions

Students said it was important for freshmen to realize that the whole college scene is new to everyone. Here are some vivid memories of first impressions:

> "My parents didn't stay long after I got moved into my room. This was good. Otherwise I would have used them to help me feel comfortable. I realized this was a completely new time for me. The first twenty minutes on my own I was extremely nervous. Then it

struck me that everyone else was too. Once I realized that, I was okay."

"My mom wanted to fly up to school with me. I thought it might look like I was too dependent, having my mother along. When I got there, all the other kids had a parent or both parents with them, helping them move in. Although there was a family friend to meet me at the airport and drop me off at the campus, it was hard moving in by myself. I had a sad feeling, knowing it would have been just fine if she had come along."

"I was excited to be going to a place where no one really knew me and I could be independent. My mom and I were taking my first set of boxes into the dorm when I heard down the hall, "Hi, Mrs. H! Is Brenda living here too?" I was crushed that someone from my high school was living two doors down from me! After two days I was kind of happy, though. There was no pressure to meet people and find someone to have dinner with or anything like that. I could go two doors down and say, 'Hey.' "

"I moved into my dorm room a week before school started, for soccer practice. So there were few people on campus. There were only two other people on a floor that normally holds fifty-three freshmen! Spending your first week away from home with little to no people around makes college a little more scary than it already was."

"I think I had a lot of buried fears about college that I wasn't in touch with at first. They didn't surface until the middle of spring my freshman year. I was riding my bike in the quad late at night. Suddenly it occurred to me that I was three thousand miles from home. I had this sink-or-swim feeling. It was scary but also exhilarating. I thought I just didn't want to ride it out the next three years. I remember telling myself: Make this an adventure. Go for it. Make new friends."

friends

Many students spoke urgently about the importance of making new friends.

"There's so much to do and figure out at first. Looking back, I wish someone would have stressed to me how important it is to begin right away to make new friends."

"I'd tell new freshmen to be more outgoing. It takes an effort, but no one is going to seek you out. If you don't go out of your way to meet new people right away, it is too easy to retreat to your room and kind of seep into the wall."

"It's important to continually seek opportunities to meet new people. Take the initiative. Don't limit

your circle of friends to just the people in your dorm
or on your floor."

"I made friends during orientation that I kept in
touch with my whole freshman year."

orientation

All schools have some form of freshman orientation. At
some colleges this may take place for two or three days during the summer. On other campuses, orientation occurs
right after students move in and lasts until classes actually
start. Its main purpose is to provide structured opportunities
to make new friends.

> "Orientation week is the real key to getting to know
> people. I remember it now as being almost as ex-
> hausting as finals week, especially if you are shy. But
> later on, when everyone gets into their own groove of
> classes and a study routine, you'll look back and see
> those were great free-time activities and events.
> You'll end up kicking yourself for not taking advan-
> tage of them when they were all set up for you."

> "We had a very intense two-day orientation. It was a
> small group, just twelve freshmen and a leader who
> was an upperclassman. We did everything together.
> Actually, it was exhausting—not a minute to your-
> self. There were short sessions on getting to know the
> campus, where everything was, what kind of majors

were offered, what kinds of clubs and extracurriculars were available. But mostly there were just a lot of
silly games to get to know each other. It felt like
being away at summer camp. And of course we ate all
our meals together. But it did work. At the end, you
felt like you had made friends that you could count
on for support. We even went to Kroger's and had a
picture of our group taken as a parting gift to our
group leader."

"We had a great orientation program that lasted
three days. There were a lot of goofy games to break
the ice. We all had to wear these ridiculous beanies.
You had to sing a song in front of everyone if you
were caught not wearing it. But it was good, as it
brought everyone down to the same level."

The Name Game

During the orientation period, several students keyed in on
remembering names.

"The single most important piece of advice I got was
how important it is to remember names. I tried to
make associations to help trigger my memory whenever I met someone new. When I went back to my
room, I wrote the name down."

"A friend who was a year older than me told me how
important it was to remember names before I went to
college. Orientation was hard for me as it is difficult
for me to be outgoing. Plus, my roommate had been a

model. We would go to the orientation things together. I remembered people's names, but no one remembered mine. Everyone remembered Susie's. I
became annoyed, having to reintroduce myself time
and time again. I had been a big fish in a small pond
in high school. Suddenly, I felt like I didn't fit in.
Also, I didn't drink. There was so much drinking. I
felt like a real geek. By Saturday, I called home in
tears. Somehow I made it through Sunday. I was very
glad on Monday when classes started. Having a
schedule helps me."

"In our freshman dorm there were so many guys
named David. So we had these T-shirts printed up
with the name of our dorm on the back, *Cheers* style:
CEDRO, A PLACE WHERE EVERYONE KNOWS YOUR NAME.
On the front, we had this little stickerlike thing
printed that said HI THERE. MY NAME IS DAVE."

feeling fragile

Several students talked about how traumatic and lonely it
can be to be thrust so totally into a very different academic
and social environment.

"It was difficult for me. I thought, no one else here is
like me. They are all different—smarter."

"I had a real fear of academics and the anxiety that I
might never see another A. I've just finished my first

semester and did well. I know I'm at that next level. It feels right. I know I belong here."

"It was difficult for me to adjust. I thought other kids seemed so much more confident of themselves—more sophisticated and cosmopolitan than me. I felt unsure of myself most of the time."

"I was painfully aware of coming from a small town. Many of the girls I met on my hall had been more places, dated more, had neater clothes, and seemed much more at ease in just routine social situations, like asking if they could sit down and eat with you in the cafeteria. It seemed easy for them to strike up conversations, like when you're in line at the bookstore. Also, they wore very expensive shoes."

"The hardest thing for me was making new friends, finding a group of people that I could connect with. I don't think I found this until my junior year. I really didn't have an idea of what community was like before I went to college."

another "i" word

When asked about advice for students who might be having problems with a particular class or studying in general, the word *initiative* kept popping up in students' responses: "You have to take the initiative to get the help you need."

When asked how they would cope with these feelings of insecurity as upperclassmen and -women, another "i" word was used in nearly every student's response. The word was *intimidated*. We asked students what advice they would want to pass on to freshmen caught up in all kinds of comparative and competitive anxiety.

"I'd say just don't let yourself be intimidated, socially or academically. Give yourself some time. You'll catch up sooner than you think. My freshman year I thought I was so different. By my senior year I thought everyone seemed pretty much the same. People catch up."

"There is so much to get used to at first. But I do remember feeling a lot more comfortable at school after the first term was over. I remember returning to college after spending the holidays at home with family. Walking into the dorm, I remember thinking, 'I'm back,' and it felt pretty good."

fraternities and sororities

In addition to dorms, many colleges have separate houses or living quarters for fraternities and sororities. At some schools, there is limited residential or off-campus housing. Fraternity and sorority houses are where the majority of students live. On other campuses, the majority of students may live in dorms or apartments, while the minority is "organized" (they belong to sororities or fraternities). Going through rush may take place during the summer, in fall after classes have started, or at the beginning of the second semester, after grades come out. Whether you decide to go through rush or not is up to you. One student said it is a good opportunity to meet people, regardless of whether you end up pledging.

> "If you aren't very outgoing, it gives you practice in being more talkative and starting up conversations: Where do you live on campus? Where's your hometown? Do you know so-and-so? What is your favorite class? Do you know what you want to major in yet?"

> "My advice? I would say it is almost impossible to be too perky when you are going through rush. I smiled until my teeth hurt."

> "Try to keep an open mind and enjoy yourself when you are going through rush. Ignore stereotypes about houses. You'll hear a lot of those when you first hit campus. Don't pay any attention to what an organization's national reputation is. The people living in the house on campus are what matter. Seek out people you like and are comfortable with. If you have to pretend to be someone you're not in order to fit in, then it's not going to be worth it."

Views of Greek Life

Those who did pledge saw the main benefit as making lasting friendships and adding a feeling of continuity to their college life.

> "Everyone in the house is there because they want to be there. It's their choice. It's a good feeling to know

my pledge brothers will be my close friends and will be there when I return again next fall."

"In addition to the continuity factor, there is always something going on at the house that I want to be a part of. Plus I like having a 'big sister' I can go and talk to when I need someone to confide in."

Others interviewed said that the fraternity or sorority provided a kind of built-in social life, an extra incentive for them to make their grades, and exposure to how college changes from year to year by providing them with opportunities to get to know the upperclassmen and -women. While fraternities especially have received much negative publicity for drinking and hazing, members are quick to point out the positive volunteer work and community projects their houses support. One senior told us, "I'm president of my fraternity this year and I don't drink. You don't have to drink to fit in."

Independent Views

Those who didn't pledge spoke about the increased cost of going Greek, plus the demands all the additional activities can put on your time. And some students think rush is just too stressful.

"I ended up de-pledging, not because I didn't like the house or the guys. I just found I couldn't work all the house activities and everything else I had to do into my schedule. It was a tough decision, though."

Another perspective from someone who still hadn't made up his mind: "A good friend of mine pledged a fraternity. He has had me over to the house for a couple of meals. They may ask me to join, but I'm not sure. It seems a very different way of life."

"I knew I was going to have to work hard to keep my scholarship and also my work-study job. So I opted to get a single room in my dorm right away and didn't pledge."

"It can be devastating if you go through rush and don't get a bid from the house you want. You feel very left out, while everyone else is very excited and celebrating. It's like being in gym class in the fourth grade again. The teams have made their picks and you're the only one left standing. By my junior year, I had moved on to other things. By your senior year you are just concentrating on finishing up and thinking about getting a job after you graduate. But when you are a freshman, well, it is a very big deal."

One student cited the whole notion of conformity and having to do what other people tell you to do during pledgeship as something he could live without. "I know I'm going to want to move into an apartment my junior or senior year, so what's the point?"

off-campus housing

In addition to dorms and fraternity and sorority houses, many campuses provide some form of off-campus housing for both single and married students. Students may decide to share apartments or rent houses or condos close to campus. If you have the choice of dorms, sororities or fraternities, or an apartment of your own, which should you choose? We asked a recent graduate for his views.

"College life is all just pretty crazy and awkward at first. You have all this instant and total freedom—it's almost scary. No one is there to tell you to go to class, study, do your laundry, or sleep. Living in a dormitory provides you with a built-in support group. You have a whole group of people you can identify with, since everyone is having to figure out and work their way through the same things. There is always someone to talk to or help you through something. There is always an R.A. who can help you sort through a problem you are having, or referee.

"Why else do I strongly support dorm life? They have all kinds of special events that are crazy and fun. And you will be thrown in and learn from a very diverse group of people. That's a big part of what college is all about."

A father who was about to send his first child off to college echoed this same thought: "I told my son I wanted him to live in a dorm his first two years. He'll never have that opportunity again, to live and mix with such a variety of people. To me, that's what you really learn from college."

One student we spoke with did live in a dorm the first two years. Then he and two friends who were also engineering majors decided to get an apartment: "We got an apartment our junior year. We all had to study a lot and wanted a quiet place. Dorms can get noisy and after a couple years you don't really need all the social life and everyone coming and going all hours of the day and night. It's worked out well for us. I think we were ready to live on our own. Also, just as dorm life helps you feel a part of college, living in an apartment will get us ready for the next step—moving out on our own after we graduate."

Another student we interviewed lived in an apartment the summer of his sophomore year, when he had a job on campus. He decided to return to the dorm for his junior year: "If you live off-campus, transportation can be a problem. But by far the biggest one is meal preparation—shopping, cooking, and cleaning up. If someone has a big exam the next day and it's his night to cook—well, it wasn't how I thought it would be. I decided it wasn't worth the hassle. Also, I got tired of eating so much spaghetti."

Another student said, "You tend to miss out on a lot of what is happening on campus when you live in an apartment. It's easy to feel very remote and unconnected to what's going on. I believe next year they are going to require first-year students to live in residence halls."

roommates

The majority of students who lived in dorms had roommates. They expressed many good ideas about the need to be
honest in the beginning—about habits or preferences in
music or TV times, computer use, late-night or early-
morning noise, visitors, and sleeping partners.

- "There's a lot to work out. You need to find a
  balance between being assertive but not being
  overly aggressive. Don't judge your roommate the
  first few days. Everyone feels a little weird at first.
  Later, it's best to deal with issues when they come
  up rather than letting it become a sore spot that
  gets blown all out of proportion."

- "I'm not a morning person, so I told my
  roommate that if I didn't say anything in the
  morning, this was normal. I wasn't mad or
  anything, just quiet."

- "I can't really add much to the roommate
  discussion. Mine went home every weekend. That
  was hard for me at first. I just ended up having to
  find other people to do things with on weekends."

- "Some kids are slobs. Then there is this guy on
  our floor who alphabetized his CDs. Nice guy. But
  not my roommate of choice."

- "There's this guy down the hall who fixed himself
  some ramen noodles, then fell asleep while he was
  eating them in bed. So he ended up with all these
  noodles dried up and stuck to his sheets, smelling
  up the room. I'm not sure if he ended up changing

his bed or if his roommate threw his sheets away."

- "My first roommate got drunk all the time. This was hard for me as I prefer to study in my room. The problem is you can't really stop anyone from drinking. It's their decision to trash themselves. One night a friend he'd been drinking with came back to the room and threw up all over my bed. I made him change everything. The next semester I got a new roommate. We roomed together for the next two years. My senior year I got a single."

- "If you're tactful and open, you can usually figure out a compromise or way to make things work out. If you can't reach a solution or you have a basic personality clash, talk to your R.A. They are there to help you with any kind of problem. They might be able to help you work it out, or you might end up switching roommates or getting a room of your own."

Home Alone

Regardless of how good a relationship you may have with your roommate, everyone needs some time alone.

"It's a good idea to coordinate times when you can have the room to yourself—to call close friends, take an uninterrupted nap, or spend a few moments in quiet reflection, meditation, or prayer."

"I guess I didn't realize how much time I'd be spending around or with people. You have roommates, people living in your hall, in your classes. It's people

24/7. You have to be very deliberate about finding privacy."

dating

There is some pairing off or hooking up, but more students talked about doing things in groups as being more comfortable. One sophomore said she felt that was a good choice:

> "It's real tempting to jump into a big serious relationship when you first get to college. Everyone is looking for security. But from my experiences, I'd recommend making as many close friends as you can—stick out the insecurity fit and don't limit yourself."

An upperclassman repeated the theme of not cutting yourself off: "People with significant others at a different school—hometown honeys—find themselves torn between two worlds. Some people advise that breaking up with your HTH is as basic as remembering to pack enough underwear. However, if a strong relationship has already been established in high school, there is a chance it will survive. Keep in mind that it is important to make the most of opportunities to meet new people your freshman year."

hanging out

Other students pointed out that doing things in groups was not only more comfortable but also less expensive.

> "It seems like no one has much money, so just hanging out is more popular than going out. Dollar movies are popular. So are all-you-can-eat buffets, where a bunch of us will go on weekends."

Students from large universities and small colleges all said that there were lots of things going on—sports, weekend film series and Sunday-night flicks, comedy, drama, music events, and lots of entertainment on campus that is either free or very inexpensive.

> "I probably didn't take good advantage of these or other things that were available—brown bag lunches with profs, special department panels, and special guest lectures. Your first year there is so much to figure out. But I do plan to take more advantage of these opportunities next fall."

> "My mother didn't tell me to study hard—just the opposite. She told me to seize the day and go see as many plays and musical performances as I could. She said that college was a rare opportunity to do these things that wouldn't be nearly as convenient or affordable later."

TIP!

Try to keep a sense of balance in your new life by hanging on to some kind of activity from your past that makes you happy or gives you joy—playing the piano or guitar, going for a run, watching a favorite video with a new friend, keeping a journal, going to a sporting event, or playing a sport.

"Don't let yourself fall into a study-eat-sleep rut."

"There is more to college than books, but there is also more than partying—don't do either too much."

"Don't just study. There are so many opportunities that exist outside of just academics. And this is coming from someone who graduated valedictorian of his high school class. Spend some time getting to know people, the local community, the city at large. Try different things that you've never thought about doing. Join an improv group. Help out with some local non-profit organizations. Don't be afraid to take risks."

"College is like Plinko. It has a beginning and it will have an end. There are all kinds of ways to bounce around in between. Try to bounce a new way. Don't just repeat the things you did or subjects you took in high school. I took philosophy instead of psychology, zoology instead of biology."

"Don't hang out with too many friends from high school. You're in a new place, so expand your horizons and the friends you make. If you start hanging out with just high school friends, you tend to fall into the same things you did back then."

"There are endless opportunities to do things I'd never even thought about, like studying abroad."

"If possible, study abroad. Go for six weeks. Maybe even spend a summer. It was one of the best experiences I ever had—really opened my eyes up to the world. It helped me mature faster than I expected. I had a blast getting to know European countries and people. It's a college experience you just can't replicate later on in life."

futures

How much time do college students spend thinking about the future? Do they talk about finding the right person and getting married? One freshman replied:

"Not really. The big question about the future is am I going to be able to find a job, have a career? People tend to start rolling their eyes if someone starts talking marriage and children. That seems a long way off."

Some students do plan ahead, however.

"I think things are changing back again. It's a scary world out there. A lot of girls talk about getting married and raising a family. It's a very big deal in our house when someone gets pinned or engaged."

Campus churches and chapels continue to be booked solid for June weddings. One tour guide explained: "I've heard that some kids aren't even going with anyone yet but have still reserved the chapel in June, just in case."

homesickness

In the midst of living with a roommate, trying to make new friends, and being constantly thrown into stressful situations and schedules, some students talked about how the adjustments to college can be overwhelming. The result is feeling homesick and longing for the familiar. Not for everyone, however.

"Not that I don't like my family. It's just that there is so much more to do here and so many more people to do it with. So I don't think much about going home."

Most of the students did talk about feeling homesick, missing all the comforts and privacy of home, and missing not being able to talk to a parent.

"It hit me hard sometimes, realizing that now my time at home would be so limited."

"I was very homesick. The first three weeks at school, I called home every other day. My mom was getting ready to come and pick me up. I'm not sure what changed, but the fourth week I began to feel settled in."

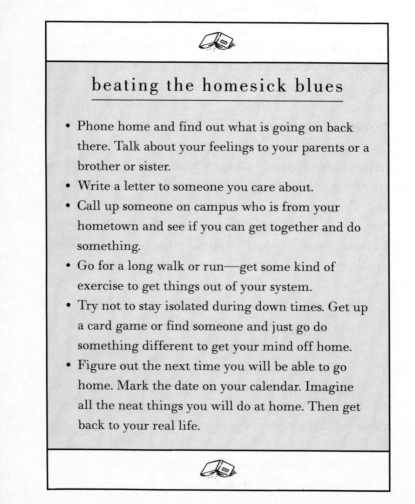

beating the homesick blues

- Phone home and find out what is going on back there. Talk about your feelings to your parents or a brother or sister.
- Write a letter to someone you care about.
- Call up someone on campus who is from your hometown and see if you can get together and do something.
- Go for a long walk or run—get some kind of exercise to get things out of your system.
- Try not to stay isolated during down times. Get up a card game or find someone and just go do something different to get your mind off home.
- Figure out the next time you will be able to go home. Mark the date on your calendar. Imagine all the neat things you will do at home. Then get back to your real life.

One student commented that one of the good things about going away was that it taught you to value your time at home with your family.

"It seems like my parents and I talk about more important things now when I'm home. I appreciate them more now."

Another student said that relationships with younger siblings can even improve, because you both realize you won't be around that much. "We both try to be a little nicer to each other than before."

"When I was at home, my younger brother and I really didn't talk that much. Now that I'm at college, we do a lot of instant messaging. Ironically, I think we have a closer relationship now."

tough transitions

Adjusting to all the changes college life brings can lead to feelings of vulnerability and anxiety. Feeling depressed can be triggered by a number of circumstances. Students described feeling overwhelmed during finals week, when so much is riding on one exam. One said it was a real blow to her when her close friend decided to leave college and return home.

Another student said he went home for Christmas looking forward to seeing his old high school friends again and things weren't the same. "They just wanted to talk about high school. I realized how things were changing. I was losing my sense of connection with them and had to let go of part of my past."

"I knew I needed to branch out and make new friends at college, but I had a tight-knit group of friends growing up in L.A. They were my real friends. My junior year my parents decided to move to Arkansas. I stayed in California. I was depressed and slept a lot. I realized I was facing a big transition and didn't know how to change. I realized I was going to have to be intentional about forming new close friendships. There was this sadness, realizing you can't go home again."

"I didn't know my freshman roommate. We were assigned roommates. He was quiet and usually came back and slept all afternoon after his classes. About all I knew about him was that he wanted to go to med school. A couple months later I met a guy from his hometown. He told me my roommate had been the real deal in high school—top jock, scholar, musician. But then just about everyone else here was from the top of his or her class, too. Maybe he was afraid he might not have the same kind of success here in this big new place. For someone who has never failed at anything, that must have been a load."

decisions

Another cause for anxiety that students expressed was having to make all your own decisions and wondering if you made the right ones: Am I taking the right classes? Should I go to class? Should I cheat on this test? What should I major in? Should I break off this relationship? Small things seem consequential.

> "I went to a small college far away from things. Merchants would come to campus selling their wares. I needed some new socks. One was selling tube socks—eight pairs for six dollars. I didn't know whether to buy them or not, if this was a good price or not. My mom always bought that kind of stuff for me. I knew nothing about managing money. You feel like you have no experience dealing with small things, let alone the really big things. There is no shelter."

> "Sometimes I felt down for no specific reason."

TIP!

Take a piece of paper and draw a line down the middle. On one side write down all the good things about your new life: what is going well, the things you enjoy about college, etc. On the other side list the areas that are causing you problems, concerns, doubts. Review those carefully to see what steps you might take to improve them. Writing things down tends to ground your thoughts. Consider sharing your "downside" list with a friend, and ask for advice.

safety nets

Every college has a counseling or student-services center staffed with professionals who are there to help students with depression or severe psychological problems. One counselor told us,

> "I think these kids have grown up in the *Oprah* culture. They seem more open about discussing personal problems they are having. At least we are seeing more of them."

It was encouraging to learn that all the students we talked with were aware that there were people on campus if they needed to unload or get help. In addition to the counseling centers, they mentioned resident assistants, academic advisers, counselors on the staff of on-campus ministries, or someone just down the hall.

> "You can always find someone to talk to if you ask. If you are in a meltdown and need someone right away, our school has a twenty-four hour hot line."

Peer Counselors

Many colleges select and train students to counsel other students. One director of student services explained, "The idea is that students are more likely to talk things over with their peers than with even the most well-intentioned adult."

We interviewed a senior who had been selected and trained for a mentoring role in a student transition program:

"I meet with a small group, between eleven and fifteen

incoming freshman, during the summer. We hold three sessions that last two days each. They do usual orientation activities like meet with their adviser, schedule their classes, learn about majors, etc. We also plan activities and create opportunities for them to get to know one another. We talk about letting go of high school and what their expectations are of college. Sometimes they put together skits and just goof off.

"Then, when they start school in the fall, I meet with the same group every Thursday, one hour a week. By then they all know one another, so we are able to have presentations and discussions on alcohol 101, date rape, anorexia/bulimia, steroid use, dating relationships, and sexual orientation. Our program has been going on for eight years. It works well, as students have a group of people they know when they first get here. And they also know I'm available to talk with them about any problems that may come up. Sometimes just having someone you trust to listen is enough to help them sort through a problem. However, if I feel they are experiencing depression or showing signs of other serious problems, I steer them toward one of the staff counselors, who is a professional therapist. My services, like theirs, are strictly confidential."

TIP!

Learn about the safety nets that are available at your school. You may need some support or may need to help a friend through a dark time.

drinking

Every student we talked to, whether attending a small private college or a large university, reported that heavy drinking is a part of college life.

> "*Party* means 'beer' here. Although major parties happen on weekends, if you want you can find a party going on somewhere any night of the week."

> "I was shocked at what a party school this was. I wanted to hide in my room and escape it and lead a very cloistered life. During Christmas break, I went to visit another campus closer to home where I knew there wasn't nearly the drinking. It would have been more comfortable to transfer. But sometimes I think it is better for you not to be too comfortable, so I came back."

> "It's hard to adjust to. You see all these really bright students, but so many of them drink. I still don't drink. After a while, you just get used to it."

> "It can be a slippery slope. Kids get carried away at first, being away from home. There is so much to drink anywhere you go. Some settle down after the first month. Others just get into the habit. I think freshmen should learn the consequences of drinking and the alternatives to it."

> "There are so many things to do here instead of drinking. My advice: Find them. My first year, since I

didn't drink, I became the designated driver. Avoid that trap. I came to resent being the person who had to take care of everybody. But drunk people don't make good decisions. I got involved in a theater group, where there were mostly upperclassmen and -women. So they were beyond the 'see how much I can drink' freshman phase. I was a lot happier then, when I got out of my caretaker role."

One student said she had felt more pressure to drink in high school than in college.

"People don't make fun of you here if you don't drink. It's not like you'll be a reject if you don't. But it is true—a lot of kids drink, a lot of the time."

Getting drunk at college certainly isn't a new phenomenon, but never have so many students—particularly women—reported binge drinking. National surveys bear out these reports. A high percentage of student deaths, academic problems, and campus rapes were found to be alcohol-related.

Colleges and universities have alcohol and drug policies but continue to seek ways to enforce them. Many have expelled fraternities from campus for alcohol-related violations. Some schools now offer substance-free dorms. Different campus groups, ministries, and organizations will sponsor parties that are publicized as alcohol-free. In Illinois, underage drinkers caught buying package liquor or drinking at a bar have to forfeit their driver's license.

While schools everywhere try to enforce substance-abuse policies, students should be aware that it will ultimately be up to them to draw the line.

"I didn't have a drink until I turned twenty-one, my
senior year. I knew my parents would hit the roof and
pull me out of here if I were busted for drinking. It
wasn't worth taking the risk."

sexual assault

We talked to two counselors at two different schools about
date rape and sexual assault. Both of them said they felt they
went largely unreported.

**"Most of the time they involve alcohol, so young
women are reluctant to come in. We go to the
dorms and hold information sessions in the first
months of school, when young women are especially vulnerable, on the dangers of alcohol, what
date rape is, how to avoid putting themselves in
dangerous situations, how they should come to the
health center right away if they think they have
been raped. We stress the dangers of sexually
transmitted diseases and try to alert everyone to
the risks and the consequences."**

Another school used students who were HIV-positive
to lead peer-panel presentations in the dorms, sororities,
and fraternities; they urged students to get tested if they
thought they could have been exposed to AIDS, and advo-
cated abstinence or using latex condoms. Some schools have
rape-awareness week early in the fall and provide a twenty-
four-hour hot line for victims. Campus newspapers continue

to write features on alcohol, drugs, and the increasing number of young women suffering from anorexia and bulimia. This is the dark side of college life that students on all campuses will be exposed to.

coping

When asked what advice he would give someone just starting college, a senior replied, "Life, especially college life, turns on a dime. Be ready for anything. Just because you are in college does not mean you are somehow inoculated from real life. Ninety-five percent of the time it is all the usual hysteria about classes, getting papers finished, or taking exams. But the other five percent is when something from the real world happens to you or your roommate or someone down the hall. A college dormitory immediately becomes a very intense, close-knit community."

A freshman expressed the same feelings. "I thought I had made good friends in high school, but it is amazing how close you become with those on your floor in such a short time. A mother of one of the girls on our floor died. We all had to deal with it together."

Indeed, nearly every student interviewed alluded to some intrusion into their college world—a tragic accident, an attempted suicide, news from home that someone in the family or a close family friend was getting a divorce or had lost her job, learning that the man who was director of the camp you worked at all last summer had died of a sudden heart attack.

"Somehow, things you've never planned on suddenly happen. You have to cope with it away from home. These are the times your relationships are so important. This is where the real learning occurs—outside the classroom."

14.

connections

You first started getting ready for college in high school. The emphasis was on selecting the right courses so that you would accumulate the academic credits you needed. It was important to perform well on SAT or ACT tests, write compelling essays, and get your applications in on time. You may have been able to squeeze in some visits to a few campuses. And you probably filled out countless financial aid and scholarship forms.

If you were on the college-bound track in high school, your guidance counselor may have even provided you with a checklist of all the steps you would need to take from your freshman year through your senior year. If you do all these things and stay on track, then you'll be ready to march down the aisle in your cap and gown. You'll pick up your diploma when they call your name, followed by whoops, claps, and cheers. With this piece of paper representing the certification of your academic credentials in your hand, you wave good-bye to your high school years. And are ready set for a brand-new chapter of your life called "College."

What's wrong with this picture? Too often, one of the most important aspects of making the transition from high school to college is totally overlooked. No one tells you how important it will be to make new friends. One freshman dean we talked to said that the single most important key to surviving the first year is for a student to find one friend to talk to, live and in person, in their new and often confusing and challenging campus environment.

"Students need to feel connected so that they can develop a sense of belonging to a new community. Rarely can they get all the support they need from family or friends at home. I tell my students to put as much time and effort into developing good friends as in making good grades."

The connections figure (see page 161) is to help you think about the people you feel connected to now—family, friends, fans. Who gives you support? Who are the people you would want to talk to or be with during your difficult and down times at college?

Fill in some of the circles with their names and you will have a picture of your personal community. There should be some empty circles. Add in the names of new people you meet at college who you think would make good friends.

Check out this picture once in a while. Have you added any new names in the new circles? Have you devoted any time or made an effort to develop these new relationships? Are you doing anything to sustain or strengthen your old friendships? If so, as you grow, so will your circle of friends, connections, and sense of belonging in your campus community.

connections

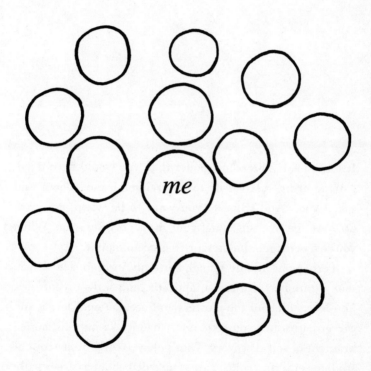

15.

career planning

It started early, probably sooner than you would have liked. An inquiring relative or total stranger leaned down and asked you, "And what do you want to be when you grow up?" At age five this is not your most pressing issue. When you're a teenager, the pressure begins to mount.

Perhaps in middle school, certainly in high school, you took a number of interest, aptitude, and skills inventories. You learned about job clusters and occupational levels and career paths. But you have never had an "a-ha, this is me" moment of self-discovery. That's okay. Nearly 50 percent of students entering college are undecided about a career path. As pointed out earlier, most colleges don't require you to declare a major until the end of your sophomore year.

How do you decide on a major? How do you discover what you really want to do after you graduate? Here are some clues for the clueless:

inquiring minds want to know

Begin by doing your own investigation. Start by asking older students:

- What are you majoring in?
- How did you decide on it?
- What are the best courses?
- Who are the good professors?
- What do you plan to do after graduation?

Talk to professors you like or those who teach a subject that interests you:

1. What led you to become a teacher?
2. What do you like about your work?
3. What aspects are the most frustrating?
4. What is academic life like outside the classroom?
5. What pressures do you face?
6. Were there any other careers you considered?
7. What are some career applications to your field outside of academia?

> ## TIP!
>
> "I would tell freshmen not to be afraid or in awe of profs. They shouldn't be. They are interested in hearing how their ideas are being received and open to questions. I've found they enjoy hearing what students think, too. Also, it's important to get to know professors. A friend of mine needs three letters of recommendation to get into graduate school. After four years, he can only come up with one prof who knows him. Don't wait until your senior year to make these important connections for grad school or for a job reference."

One professor we spoke to said he was always surprised that students didn't see that getting to know a professor is a good way of advancing their interest in a class. "That's why we have office hours. It bothers me when a student comes in for a discussion and then before he or she leaves says, 'Thanks for your time.' My response is always, 'Don't thank me, this is my job.' "

TRUE STORY

"I didn't have the opportunity to take psychology in high school, yet I knew I wanted to do some kind of work in counseling. I was disappointed when all the Psych 101 classes were full, as I was eager to get started. (Sometimes you can't always get into a course you want right away.) However, my second semester I got in. I really loved the class and my professor.

"I took the initiative to get to know her and told her I thought I was especially interested in teenage depression. She wrote a recommendation to a colleague of hers who was doing work in that area. It was only my sophomore year, and here I was helping her with her research project by interviewing disturbed teens. I could hardly believe it! I even ended up earning credits toward my major. If I hadn't made it a point to get to know my first prof and talk to her, I would have missed this wonderful opportunity."

information, please

In addition to seeking out information from friends and professors, continue to gather occupational data by interviewing other people about what they do for a living—parents, relatives, neighbors. After you've practiced with people you're comfortable with, you can begin to branch out and uncover firsthand job information from individuals you don't know. Most adults will be flattered that you are interested in their work. Also, people who like what they do usually enjoy talking about it. Here's a sample script:

I'm trying to figure out what I want to be when I grow up. Would you mind telling me about your job?

- What are the good things about your work?
- What parts do you enjoy?
- What kinds of problems do you encounter?
- What is a bad day at work like?
- What key skills does your job require?
- What kinds of things do you just learn on the job?

- What advice would you give to someone new?
- If you could be doing anything now, what would it be? [You will get some really interesting responses to this one.]

Get in the habit of asking these questions of new people you meet. Then ask yourself: Does this sound like something I'd like to do?

the x-files

Another fairly painless method for collecting information about yourself involves buying two large folders, one for pictures—ads, photos, illustrations—and one for words— newspaper or magazine articles, campus flyers, etc. Begin to randomly clip, save, and file away in either folder anything that grabs your eye or interests you. Later, empty the contents and spread the articles out or create a collage of the pictures. Look for patterns, ideas, themes, connections. The truth is in there.

the "major" question

All of this exploration can be interesting and can generate new ideas and possibilities, but at some point in your college career you will have to declare a major. Should you major in a subject you really like and take your chances of being able to find a job after graduation? Or should you select a field of study that is more likely to lead to a job or career? You may be very interested in art or anthropology, but would it be more practical to major in accounting? Which is the best path to follow?

"follow your bliss"

This phrase, which means to study something you love and let your interests and passions guide you, was the advice of Joseph Campbell, a famous teacher. (His *The Power of Myth*, an old but excellent PBS video series, would be well worth checking out from your local library. Pretend you are in Campbell's class. Practice taking notes.) Many would agree that you might as well choose a major you can enjoy. Why? The job market is changing very rapidly. By the time you graduate, the unpredictable economy might be in the best of times or the worst of times. Plus, studies indicate that young adults should now figure on having four to six different careers in their lifetime. So a broad liberal arts background might be a better choice in the long run than a more narrowly focused or job-specific major. Learning to think for yourself by examining issues and ideas, asking the right questions, connecting them with the world around you, and communicating your thoughts in a clear and responsible way—these are the kinds of broad skills you can learn in any major. They are also skills that are marketable in the workplace.

real life 101

Consider the amount of time in your life you will spend working—80,000 hours is a figure commonly used. Finding something you really enjoy doing and someone to pay you to do it is certainly the best career advice there is.

Also, have you noticed that people who like what they do are usually good at it? Consider Dick Vitale. Do you think he has to haul himself out of bed in the morning to get ready to broadcast a basketball game, force himself to go to the gym, hobnob with the players, have lunch with the General? Certainly not! He exhibits a passion and curiosity for everything connected with basketball. He may drive you crazy, but he clearly loves his work. And that's one good way to keep score.

People who are not happy in their work—and surveys tell us this is well over half the population—sometimes unhook themselves from what they do for a living, declaring, "My day begins at five P.M." That can be a good coping device. But the problem with it is that it makes for very short days.

rolling stones

People who like their work see it as an extension of themselves or something they care about.

There is the old tale about three men walking down a road carrying stones. When stopped and asked what he was doing, the first man grumbled, "I'm carrying stones." The second man was asked the same question. He calmly replied, "I'm carrying stones so that I can earn money to take care of my wife and child." When the third man was asked what he was doing he whispered, "I'm building a cathedral." Same job. Different perspectives.

follow the bucks

The flip side of the "follow your bliss" coin is to pursue a more practical path, one that will lead directly to a specific occupation. There are many good reasons to choose this route—food, shelter, student loans to be paid off. Let's face it. Corporations have never lined up on campuses in droves to hire art history or international peace majors, even in the best of times. Technical graduates or those with a specific career field have the clear edge when it comes to immediate job opportunities. And again, projecting ahead that you will have four to six careers in your lifetime, you may as well start out with one that provides you with core competencies. So if you know you will be looking for a job as soon as you graduate, then it makes sense to position yourself so that the knowledge and experiences you acquire in college will be most immediately marketable when you get out.

help abounds

I hope this section has been helpful. But don't think you'll have to make all these decisions on your own. Your school's career-planning center will have a wealth of very current information on the job market and outlook. There are counselors to help you with assessment tools, interest inventories, business resources, and the latest scoop on preparing résumés.

> **TIP!**
>
> Pay a visit to the career center
> before your junior year.

final thoughts

Majors and graduation may seem a long way off. But after you struggle through and survive your first year, the following years will go quickly.

Make sure to keep track of your credit hours. Continue to check with your adviser to make sure you are taking the requirements and credit hours you will need to graduate. We recommend you do this at the end of each school year. This is especially important if you switch majors or transfer from another school.

Advisers make mistakes. Requirements for a certain major may change during your four years. Don't rely on hearsay. Insist on finding someone to help you if you have any doubts or questions about the number and kinds of credits you will need to graduate. We've heard too many very sad stories of students finding out at the last minute they couldn't graduate because they were short required hours or courses.

TRUE STORY

I asked one student if he was having too much fun or not enough fun at college. He replied, "My parents keep telling me these are the best years of my life. I find that depressing.

Last fall I sold programs at the homecoming football game and watched all those alums come smiling in, looking so happy to be back. Maybe I'm missing something. Or maybe they are. It's hard to tell, isn't it?"

16.

jobs 101

What's the best way to prepare yourself for the job market? Getting some hands-on work experience before you graduate will be invaluable.

All the students we interviewed held part-time jobs during high school and worked full-time at a job or jobs during the summer. After surviving their first year of college, they returned to work. Once again they became retail clerks, lifeguards, waitresses, assembly-line workers, baby-sitters, and recreation directors. After a summer back in the temporary workforce, they headed back to campus to begin their sophomore year with some new perspectives.

back to the books

One student studying engineering worked the first shift in a factory all summer. "We worked every day from six-thirty until two-thirty, with twenty minutes for lunch, with a ten-minute break every two hours—five days a week. I realized how much time I had wasted during the day at college, especially between classes. I see my class work just like a job now. I leave the dorm and head for the library at eight A.M. even if my first class isn't until noon. That's still an hour and a half later than when I started work in the plant."

Another young woman spent her summer waiting tables in a busy upscale restaurant. While the tips were good, her feet grew weary. She vowed to become more committed to doing well in her studies when she returned to college: "I want to get accepted into law school when I graduate."

A third young man had what most college students dream about—a real internship in the area of his major. It actually had a salary attached to it, too. (Don't laugh. Many big-time companies have students scrambling for unpaid internships. Why? Students want to gain experience and get a foot in the door.) This student had dreamed of being an architect.

"I was thrilled to get an internship with a small firm," he said. "I had my own office, a great computer, and a stack of designs. But after a month I realized I wasn't cut out to work at a computerized drawing board all day. I missed being with people."

When he returned to campus in the fall, he went to see his counselor. Together they mapped out a plan to combine his love of sports and some great communication skills into a sports-administration major. After graduation he took a temporary job promoting a seniors' golf tournament. While working the tournament he made some good contacts, which resulted in a full-time marketing position with the Indianapolis 500.

iq vs. eq

Jobs are great teachers. If nothing else, you may learn what it is that you *don't* want to do. You can also make discoveries in the world of work that wouldn't be possible in the class-room. For example, in college you may run into a class taught by a prof you have problems with. He or she is too hard to understand, unclear about expectations, too de-tached, doesn't seem to grade fairly, or is just plain boring. Still, it is possible to disregard these feelings. You move the class from your mental dread zone into a more neutral time zone. You tell yourself you are just going to keep plugging away because it will be over within a short time. You just have to hang in there until the end of the semester and it will be over with.

However, if this kind of person turns out to be your full-time boss, you will need to develop some nonacademic survival skills. Daniel Goleman's groundbreaking book *Emotional Intelligence* explores the emphasis that has been put on the importance of IQ. He maintains that having a strong EQ, or emotional intelligence, may be a more de-termining factor than IQ in leading a successful or happy life.

The basic skills of emotional intelligence, governed by a different circuit in the brain, lie in the areas of being aware of your feelings and having empathy for others. How do you manage your feelings, deal with conflict, interact with other people, react to unfair situations, respond to unspoken feel-ings, deal with your disappointments or other people's suc-cess? How easy is it for you to go along with someone else's plan if you think yours is a better one? These are the kinds of nitty-gritty things you can learn about yourself in the workplace.

testing the waters

In addition to testing your emotional intelligence, summer or temporary jobs are an excellent way to test occupational waters. They can provide an opportunity to do a reality check and see if you enjoy being in a particular work atmosphere. Even the most menial jobs in a hospital, law firm, police department, press room, bank, radio or TV station, or business office will give you access to the environment, people, and language. You'll get to discover on your own what work is like in these places and not have to rely on versions presented on TV.

Also, any practical work experience will give you an edge when you begin looking for permanent employment, especially if it is related to your career interests. One career counselor we interviewed said she urges students to be proactive: "Initiative is so important. Students need to find some experience hooks to hang their knowledge on. I tell them to look for a way to create a summer work experience if one isn't readily available."

volunteer!

Look around your community. Who needs help? Nearly all non-profits, like Habitat for Humanity, can use young, energetic volunteers. Depending on your skills or interests, you could offer to write or produce a newsletter, create a new brochure or mailing to be used in an upcoming fund drive, see if an agency could use some help computerizing or formatting a budget or donor-tracking form. You could develop leadership experience by volunteering to head up a special fund-raising event for a favorite charity in your town.

There are many volunteer groups to help young people. Most towns and cities have summer programs to help kids improve their reading skills. Or you could lead a recreational activity at a local YMCA or Boys' or Girls' Club.

One student who plans to be a social worker is also a licensed aerobics instructor: "There are so many kids at risk needing help and attention. I lead a summer aerobics class for them. It's brand-new to them, but they enjoy it and we have a good time."

résumés

Don't think that because you won't get paid for volunteer work you aren't earning anything. You are. In addition to making personal contacts, volunteer efforts also qualify as work experience when you get ready to prepare your résumé. Think of your résumé as a one-page personal advertisement—your best self on paper. Along with the traditional information—academics, campus activities, and work experience—a résumé should name your key skills and personal strengths. What makes you unique? What do you want to tell someone about yourself in an interview?

The Internet is packed with job and career sites. However, don't plan on creating a great résumé, posting it on the Web, and waiting for an employer to beam you up into a job from cyberspace. Prepare a résumé with the purpose of getting a face-to-face interview with an employer. People still hire people, not résumés.

star power

When you do get an interview, it's important to be able to name your key strengths or skills. What are the three things you do best? What skills can you sell to a future employer? These could involve a specific technical expertise you've learned in school or general skills you've developed on your own. Are you dependable, energetic, creative, good at problem solving, skilled at managing your time, showing initiative, coming up with practical solutions? All of these are very marketable skills and strengths. The key is to learn to describe them effectively.

Think of situations that demonstrate your skills, strengths, or traits. Use the STAR (Situation–Took Action–Result) technique as a way to provide an example. State the situation or set of circumstances when you used a particular skill, what you did, and what you accomplished. Think of it as creating a sixty-second infomercial starring yourself. Keep it short and sweet. Rehearse it. And of course, in telling it in an interview, be spontaneous!

Never turn down a chance for an interview. Selling yourself involves identifying what you do best and giving examples with short STAR stories. Gaining self-confidence requires effort and enthusiasm. Most of all, it takes persistence and practice. What do you do after you've landed a job? For some expert advice, keep reading.

on-the-job tips

How well you perform in your college classes is largely up to you. You may collaborate with others for a few group projects or form a study group. However, most of the time the grade you receive in a course represents your individual effort.

The world of work is different. There are different ways of grading, different kinds of challenges. Your performance will depend on less-tangible factors than getting a high score on a test. Two of the keys for success in a work setting revolve around establishing a good relationship with your boss and working effectively with the people around you.

Christine Letts knows a lot about both. She is currently with the Hauser Center of Nonprofit Organizations at Harvard University. She gave the following advice at an orientation for new college employees while serving as vice president of operations at Cummins Engine Company. Review her tips before you start a new summer job, an internship, or your first full-time position.

On Bosses

- Work hard to get along with your boss.
- Get as smart as you can on what you'll be discussing with him/her.
- Think of some good questions to ask.
- Don't confront—listen.
- Learn to influence, not confront.
- Until you gain some credibility, go with your boss's plan.

- Help your boss be successful.
- After a while, don't be afraid to ask, "Do you want to solve this problem?"

On Managing Yourself

- Don't go out of your way to get exposure, but when you have the limelight, be prepared so that you present your ideas well.
- Don't complain. Be positive. Be optimistic. Don't whine. (This is hard!)
- Think about making positive change rather than being right.
- Seek advice.
- Work hard in your current job. Learn the basic competencies.
- Be concise.
- Offer solutions.

On Becoming Part of the Team

- Help your peers.
- Figure out how you can have influence, regardless of your position in the organizational structure.
- Influence is gained through knowledge, credibility, and trust.
- Don't be seen as an obstacle when you walk into a meeting. Be seen as a helper.
- Be prepared to make compromises but not too many in a row.

- Try to keep your options open rather than closing them off.

On Soliciting Feedback

- In college you receive a grade for your work; this tells you how you are doing.
- At work, you may need to ask for feedback on your performance.
- After you've been on the job for a while, ask your boss, peers, and human resource person: How am I doing? Am I focusing on the right things? Where do I need to improve? How do I come across?

On Finding the Balance

- Keep a balance between patience and urgency.
- Be patient with people. Respect where they are.
- Be urgent with things.
- Think more about serving than leading.
- Every job is an opportunity to learn something.
- Experience is something you get when you are expecting something else.

On Hours

- You need to strike a balance between your work life and your outside life.

- Put in extra hours at work when the work needs to be done.
- Very long hours should only be necessary sporadically; don't let them become your norm.
- Nurture the other side of your life.
- Organize your leisure time.
- Keep your life full.
- Become more than your job.

17.

dining-out tips

Perhaps your roommate's parents ask you to join them for dinner at a nice restaurant or a guest speaker comes to campus and you're invited to attend a special luncheon after the lecture. Or maybe you are into a serious job hunt and your interview day includes a lunch break with someone from the company. Here are a dozen dining-out tips that may come in handy.

Seating—After a waiter shows you to the table, it's polite to stand behind a chair until the host asks you to sit. He or she may have a seating arrangement in mind. If it isn't clear where you belong, just ask the host, "Is there anyplace special you would like me to sit?"

Napkins—Place your napkin on your lap after everyone is seated. If you need to excuse yourself from the table—to use the rest room or for extended coughing or blowing your nose—leave your napkin on your chair. Don't place your used napkin on the table until it's time to leave.

Menus—It's a good idea to ask your host what he recommends. This will give you some idea of the price range. If no clues are given, just order something that's in the middle range—not the most or least expensive item on the menu.

TIP!

If you're in a job interview, avoid ordering something that you've never tried before or a dish that might be messy or awkward to eat. Also be aware: Your host may say, "Well, now it's time to just relax and take a break in your schedule." You are still being interviewed—just a little less formally.

Follow the Leader—The easiest rule to remember when dining out is simply to follow the host or person at the head of the table. Begin to eat after he or she does. If you're not sure when or how to eat something, just watch and follow the leader. If your host uses a knife and fork to eat chicken, french fries, or pizza, you should do the same.

Silverware—Start from the outside and work in. It's that simple. A soup spoon will be the farthest to the right. Use the fork farthest to the left for whatever may be served first—fish, salad, etc. A spoon or fork placed near the top of the plate is meant for dessert. If you drop a piece of silverware, leave it on the floor and ask the waiter or waitress for a replacement. If a piece of food slides off your plate onto the floor, don't make a big deal out of it. This happens. Just leave it there.

Soup—In order to avoid dripping, you should spoon away from yourself rather than toward yourself. Don't slurp or crunch up a bunch of crackers in your soup. Place the soup spoon on the plate beneath the bowl when you are finished.

Pass Right—Rolls and other items are usually passed to the right. The host should start the passing process. If not, feel free to request what you need. Ask for an item to be passed instead of reaching across the table for it.

Butter Bits—Break off a small piece of bread or roll and butter it while it is on the plate. Then pick it up and eat it. Don't butter the whole thing all at once or butter it in midair.

Taste Test—Don't automatically salt and pepper food or add a table sauce to your food. Taste it first to see if it needs it. The chef may have gotten it just right.

Cut-ups—Don't cut up your meat all at one time. Cut only one piece and then eat it before cutting another. Repress your inner child, who may tell you to eat all your meat, then all your corn, then all your rice, etc.

Timing—Don't talk with your mouth full. (You may have heard this one before.) Swallow first, even if this means an awkward pause while someone waits for your response to a question.

TIP!

Miss Piggy had it right: Don't eat more than you can lift. Take small bites. Take a drink after you have swallowed your food, not during.

Pacing and Patience—Try to pace your eating with that of others at the table.

TRUE STORY

I once asked an old-guard British host why he hadn't cleaned his plate.

"Oh, I never do," he said. "I always leave a little food to push around on my plate so that slow eaters are never embarrassed to be the last ones finished. Good manners are simply making other people feel comfortable."

18.

how to build a loft

The following standards for building a loft are considered minimum. To ensure a safe structure, these specifications should be strictly met or exceeded. The weight limitation should not exceed 500 pounds total weight.

general loft
requirements and definitions

Loft
The raised platform constructed according to regulations; the completed structure.

All lumber used in loft construction must be kiln-dried and properly seasoned. "Green" lumber, tree limbs, etc., are not permitted. Cracked wood is not acceptable. Number 1 kiln-dried wood is permissible.

Vertical Supports

The vertical members designed to hold up the deck of a completed loft.

Supports must be free-standing (not attached to walls, closets or the building). They are to be made of 4″ × 4″'s (see Example A) OR 2″ × 4″'s glued and bolted together of sufficient length (see Example B), and are needed at every corner.

Cross Beams

The horizontal members attached to the supports, designed to hold the deck joists and deck.

Cross beams are to be of 2″ × 6″ material and cannot exceed 40 inches in length. They are to be bolted to each support with two carriage bolts ⅜″ × 4″ in size and with two washers plus a lock washer and nut for each bolt. (See Examples A and B.)

Cross Supports

Required along the back side of the structure to strengthen the loft. These two cross supports are 2″ × 4″'s attached diagonally at opposing angles. They are affixed to the supports at the back side of the structure by bolts, washers, and nuts. The bottom of the low end of the cross support is to be 6″ above the floor. The top of the high end is to be 6″ below the bottom of the juncture of the cross beams and the supports. One cross support will be mounted on the outside of the vertical supports, the other on the inside. Two horizontal 2″ × 4″ supports are required, one at each end of the loft to further strengthen it. They are to be secured by bolts, washers, and nuts. The top edge of each horizontal support is to be 12″ above the floor and mounted on the inside of the vertical supports. (See Example C.)

Top Platform Supports

Required to support the loft platform. These three 2″ × 4″'s are mounted on (nailed on) joist hangers to cross beams to support a ¾″ plywood sheet. The plywood sheet is screwed to these supports and cross beams. (See Example D.) NOTE: Particle board or other materials are not acceptable substitutes for plywood.

materials needed

The materials needed to construct a loft utilizing Example A (4″ × 4″ supports) are listed on Materials List A.

The materials needed to construct a loft utilizing Example B (2″ × 4″ supports) are listed on Materials List B.

materials list a

$4' \times 8' \times \frac{3}{4}''$ plywood	1 each	platform
$2'' \times 6'' \times 8'$	1 each	cross beam
$2'' \times 4'' \times 8'4''$	each platform	cross support and end cross support
$2'' \times 4'' \times 10'$	2 each	back cross support
$4'' \times 4'' \times$ height	4 each	vertical supports
$2'' \times 4''$ joist hangers	6 each	platform cross supports
bolts $\frac{3}{8}''$— 16 threads per inch $\times 4''$	20 each	
bolts $\frac{3}{8}''$— 16 threads per inch $\times 6''$	12 each	
flat washers $\frac{3}{8}''$	64 each	
lock washers $\frac{3}{8}''$	32 each	
$\frac{3}{8}''$ nuts 16 threads per inch	32 each	
#8 $\times 1''$ round head wood screws	36 each	joist hangers
#8 $\times 2''$ flat head wood screws	19 each	plywood platform
waterproof carpenter's glue		

materials list b

4′ × 8′ × ¾″ plywood	1 each	platform
2″ × 6″ × 8′	1 each	cross beam
2″ × 4″ × 8′	4 each	platform cross support and end cross support
2″ × 4″ × 10′	2 each	back cross support
2″ × 4″ × height	8 each	vertical cross support
2″ × 4″ joist hangers	6 each	platform cross support
bolts ⅜″— 16 threads per inch × 4″	20 each	
bolts ⅜″— 16 threads per inch × 6″	12 each	
flat washers ⅜″	64 each	
lock washers ⅜″	32 each	
⅜″ nuts— 16 threads per inch	32 each	
#8 × 1″ round head wood screws	36 each	joist hangers
#8 × 2″ flat head wood screws	19 each	plywood platform
waterproof carpenter's glue		

example a

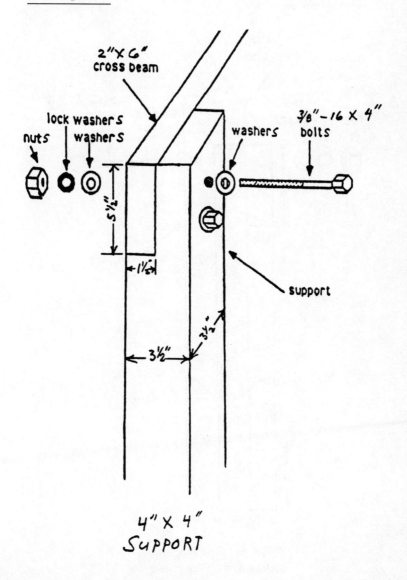

2"×6"
cross beam

lock washers
washers

nuts

washers

3/8"−16 × 4"
bolts

5½"

1½"

support

3½"

3½"

4" × 4"
SUPPORT

example b

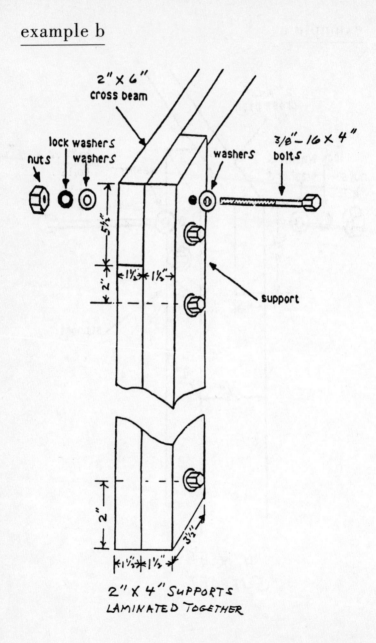

2" × 6"
cross beam

lock washers
washers

nuts

3/8"– 16 × 4"
bolts

washers

support

5½"

2"

1½" 1½"

2"

3½"

1½" 1½"

2" × 4" SUPPORTS
LAMINATED TOGETHER

example c

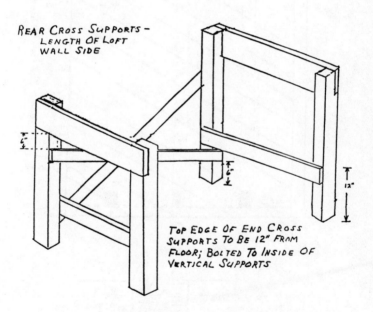

REAR CROSS SUPPORTS –
LENGTH OF LOFT
WALL SIDE

12"

TOP EDGE OF END CROSS
SUPPORTS TO BE 12" FROM
FLOOR; BOLTED TO INSIDE OF
VERTICAL SUPPORTS

example d

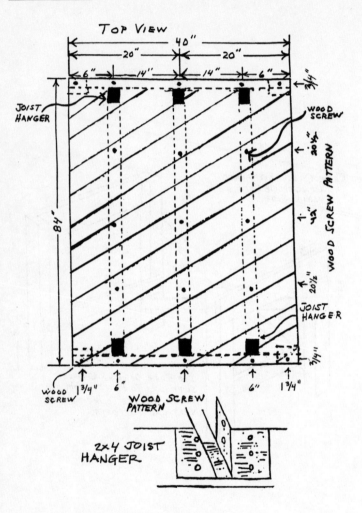

building and transporting tips

Many students we have talked to make building a loft their summer project. We have heard good stories that indicate that working on this project together with a parent, grandparent, or some avid *Home Improvement*–fan neighbor provides a nice bonding experience. They build it at home, then take the loft apart, keep the directions, pack it in the van, and then reassemble it when they get on campus.

If you will be driving a pickup truck, you can load the loft on the bed and pack the other things you are taking with you underneath it.

If you will be flying up and away to college, you can take these directions with you and build one or pay someone to build one for you once you arrive. (Materials will not fit in the overhead rack or under your seat.)

Some students add personal touches of their own. They add ladders or small shelflike platforms on top to hold a clock radio or alarm clock. Others paint their loft to fit in with their room décor. Most students are apt to develop a strong attachment to their loft and decide to bequeath it to a younger brother or sister. Many take the loft with them when they move into a cramped apartment. So a loft can prove to be a good and practical investment, with a long after-college life of its own.

19.

things to think about

My first job after college was teaching English in a high school in Indianapolis. My senior students were all bound for college. They were very bright. And very bored. Everything seemed dull and gray to them—school, the social scene, who's in, what's out, silly rules, dumb restraints. They weren't hostile, just disengaged.

One phrase kept cropping up in their weekly themes: "When I get out into real life . . ." By November I began to think of this as the Pinocchio phenomenon. It was as if these eighteen-year-olds saw themselves as puppets, leading stiff and wooden lives, and were ready to break the strings that manipulated them.

Suddenly, at some magic point in the future, they would spring miraculously to life, jumping and shouting with joy. Transformed, they would finally exclaim, "I'm a real boy!" "I'm a real girl!" Then I would leave them dancing around in my head and get back to my own real life. I would seize my red Flair pen, circle the phrase, and write vigorously in the margin: LIFE DOESN'T GET MUCH "REALER" THAN WHEN YOU ARE EIGHTEEN!

How about you? Did you suffer from senioritis? If you are still in high school and find yourself bored and listless, spend some time thinking back over your high school years. Bring them into focus. Consider the questions below. It's one of the best things anyone can do to get ready for college. And it doesn't cost a cent.

1. College isn't a popularity contest. Grades matter. How much time did you spend studying? (Remember, we are considering all four years now.) Which class was your hardest? In which class did you do your best work? Which class was your favorite? When did time fly? Was it because of the subject, the teacher, or the participation of other kids in the class? When were you bored to tears?

2. How about all the extracurriculars you listed in your college applications: sports, clubs, committees, volunteer work. What gave you the most satisfaction? What was the most fun? Did you overbook yourself? Is there anything you wish you had tried out for in high school but didn't? What kinds of activities do you see yourself repeating or exploring in college?

3. Who are your best friends? How did you meet them? Did you hang out with the same kids all four years, or did your friends change? Was there

anyone in a different group you would have liked
to get to know better but didn't? Why not? What
held you back?

4. Remember your happy times. Imagine that you
are going to make your own high school
highlights tape. What memories would you
include? What real-life moments still sparkle in
your mind? When did your going-through-the-
motions world turn from gray into gold? When
did you feel most completely yourself?

5. Looking back, what were some of your
disappointments? (But don't tape these!) What do
you think you missed out on? How do you want
your college life to be different from your high
school days? What can you do to make that
happen? Think hard about this one.

College is a brand-new slate. You can make new choices,
seek a better balance. One girl majored in cheerleading in
high school, got serious about studies in college, and amazed
everyone by making a GPA of 4.0 her senior year. Another
guy had gone the nerd route in high school, already adopt-
ing a "med school or bust" mind-set. In college he made
making friends and developing relationships a new priority.
Whatever choices you make, appreciate having them. The
U.S. Census of March 2000 found that 26 percent of Americans age twenty-five or older have a bachelor's degree.
Think about joining those ranks. Yet remember the words
of Seymour's most famous son, John Mellencamp: Your life
is now.

20.

postscript to parents

There were two productions that spoke to my generation—the movie *The Graduate* and the Broadway musical *Hair*. I remember sitting with friends in a dark theater, wearing my tapestry vest and bell-bottom jeans, waiting for the movie we had heard so much about to begin. In the opening scene, Dustin Hoffman is being hailed as a new college graduate at a party his parents are giving in his honor.

They and their country-club friends are in happy spirits, congratulating him on his academic honors and speculating about his bright future. Dustin is mostly walking around with his hands in his pockets or staring into the aquarium, not exactly wired into the social reality. One of his parents' friends pulls him away from the crowd to give him some career advice. As if he is about to share with him the ultimate secret of the universe, he whispers one word into Hoffman's ear—"Plastics!" I remember how we all exploded with laughter, thinking it had to be one of the best lines ever written.

And yet twenty-five years later, I found myself button-holing my own nineteen-year-old son and doing exactly the same thing. When it came time for him to choose a major, I was just as urgently whispering the words *computers* or *engineering*. I didn't even question my right to prescribe his future. I was a lot older and wiser. As a single parent, I was doubly entitled to know what was best for him. Also, I meant well. All my sighs and whispers were coming from somewhere inside me where there was a deep wanting—to steer him out on a safer, smoother, and perhaps saner journey.

Perhaps as parents you will find yourself in a similar situation. You will want your son or daughter to attend the college of your dreams, major in something you think makes great practical sense, join a sorority or fraternity or not join one, and land a job after graduation that holds the promise of security and financial success: You want a return on your investment.

It is so easy to become overly invested in the key decisions your child will be making in the college years ahead. It is also easy to find yourself living vicariously through your child's new experiences. You are hardly alone. Because so many parents struggle with these issues, some college orientation programs are now offering sessions "for parents only." I highly recommend *Letting Go: A Parents' Guide to Understanding the College Years,* by Karen Coburn and Madge Treeger. It can guide you through the hills and valleys ahead.

While learning to let go may be the toughest assignment for parents, it is the only way young adults will be able to get out into that real life they have so long imagined: no strings, jumping for joy, filled with their own dreams and discoveries.

The musical *Hair* featured mostly naked twenty-somethings jumping around onstage, joyfully ushering in the Age of Aquarius. In the midst of all this youthful exuberance, there is this mother in the audience who leaps up on the stage, clutching her plastic pocketbook as she delivers her urgent message: "Now, kids, do whatever you do, be whatever you want to be, as long as you don't hurt anybody. And, remember. I am your friend."

Now, thirty years later, that seems to me to be one of the best lines ever written.

acknowledgments

I am greatly indebted to all the students I've interviewed over the past ten years. It was a privilege to listen and record your stories. I will always appreciate your openness, wit, and honesty.

I also owe a collective thanks to the professors, deans, counselors, and health care professionals at Indiana University, De Pauw University, Hanover College, Franklin College, and Stanford University. Your detailed information and insights on how you interact with students provided me with a much fuller picture of campus life.

A very special thanks to my editors, Ivan Held, Veronica Windholz, and Danielle Durkin, and to the design staff at Random House. Your enthusiasm and expertise turned a very plain self-published text into a real live book.

There are lots of relatives who deserve special recognition: my son, Jonathan Berent, whose many college experiences and adventures finally drove me to take pen in hand;

and his wife, Jeanne, for sharing her great financial expertise in an important new section of this book; nephews Dave and Matt Dittmer, for their many timely updates and always entertaining outtakes on all things college; John Dittmer, the real writer in the family, for his early interest in this project and continued guidance; his wife, Ellen, who rounded up a great new group of students for me to interview; Stan Dittmer and Sally Fenton, for the wonderful memories of their California hosting, which allowed me to go to college once a year. And Randy Dittmer and Patty Dittmer Cress, whose ongoing encouragement on the home front has always been greatly appreciated.

I would like to take this opportunity to express my gratitude to Maureen O'Hara Pesta, Beth Schulte, Herb and Nancy Brown, and the Park House guys—Rich, Jim, and Dominique. Your friendship and encouragement have been extraordinary.

Most of all, there are two people who deserve special thanks. My youngest brother, Tony Dittmer, is the computer wizard who made the early editions of this manuscript a reality, cranking them out on his mythical Moon Shadow Press. His expertise and judgment were reflected in every original page. Tony always got it right, with patience and humor. I am also very grateful to Katie Hall, whose efforts and endorsement rallied the needed support for this book. She encouraged me to explore important new areas, which greatly broadened the scope and depth of our manuscript. Katie's insight and grace made everything new.

index

POLLY BERENT has a degree in comparative literature from Indiana University. She has been a high school English teacher, a flight attendant, an overseas volunteer for the Thomas A. Dooley Foundation in Laos and Cambodia, and a human resources manager for a Fortune 500 company. She has conducted college and career workshops throughout the Midwest. Berent self-published *Getting Ready for College* for the first time in 1993. She has one son and lives in Seymour, Indiana.